PRICING
FOR
PROFIT

PRICING
FOR
PROFIT

How to Command Higher Prices
for Your Products and Services

Dale Furtwengler

AMACOM

American Management Association
New York • Atlanta • Brussels • Chicago • Mexico City
San Francisco • Shanghai • Tokyo • Toronto • Washington, D.C.

This publication is designed to provide accurate and authoritative information in regard to the subject matter covered. It is sold with the understanding that the publisher is not engaged in rendering legal, accounting, or other professional service. If legal advice or other expert assistance is required, the services of a competent professional person should be sought.

Library of Congress Cataloging-in-Publication Data

Furtwengler, Dale.
    Pricing for profit : how to command higher prices for your products and services / by Dale Furtwengler.
        p. cm.
    Includes bibliographical references and index.
    ISBN 978-0-8144-1517-7
    1. Pricing. 2. Markup. 3. Marketing. I. Title.
    HF5416.5.F87   2010
    68.8′16—dc22
                                                                                        2009014406

PRINTING NUMBER

10 9 8 7 6 5 4 3 2 1

Contents

Acknowledgments

None of us accomplishes anything worthwhile without the support and encouragement of others. That's why I want to take a few moments to thank the people who have supported me over the years.

To Charlotte, my wife, whose love supports, encourages, and sustains me in every thing I do. You have the wonderful ability, with your loving smile, to make everything right with the world. Words cannot express my joy and appreciation for the love and support you've given me over the past thirty-five years, the best of my life. Thank you.

I was given a tremendous leg up in life by my parents, Charles and Johanna Furtwengler. They taught my brothers and me to be independent and to go after whatever we wanted from life. Finally, they believed in us so that we could believe in ourselves. These gifts are priceless and continue to serve us today. Mom and Dad, thank you for your love and wisdom.

I'd like to thank all of the clients I've worked with over the years for helping me gain the knowledge necessary to help others become more successful in their businesses. It's through these experiences that I'm able to provide field-tested concepts to help you, the reader. A special thanks to all of my clients, present and past, for helping me grow personally.

Family and friends are always an essential element to one's success. I've had the good fortune not only to have been born into a loving family, but to marry into one as well. I've also been blessed with friends who are cheerleaders, not just for me, but for everyone they meet. Their numbers are legion and too numerous to mention here. You know who you are. Thank you for all you do to make this world a better place.

In 2000, Jessica Faust was an acquisitions editor for Macmillan Publishing. She found me and offered me my first book contract. Jessica and her partner, Jacky Sach, have since formed their own company, BookEnds LLC. Jessica artfully guided me through the process of submitting and gaining acceptance of this book concept. Thank you, Jessica. I couldn't have done it without you.

Good fortune continued for me as I was introduced to and began to work with my editor, Bob Nirkind. Bob is the kind of editor every author dreams of having. One who is encouraging, insightful, and an excellent communicator in his own right. Bob's suggestions have proven invaluable and the enhancements he made to the readability of this book accrue to your benefit. Thank you, Bob, for a truly enjoyable experience.

May all of you enjoy all the best life has to offer!

PRICING FOR PROFIT

Introduction

"I can't raise prices; I won't be competitive." This belief represents one of the greatest frustrations business owners experience. One homebuilder spent 45 minutes telling me why his homes were better than his competitors'. Yet he didn't feel that he could raise prices, even though his prices were 10 percent below market.

How does this happen? Why do businesspeople feel trapped by industry pricing even though they know, with absolute certainty, that their offerings are superior? *They don't know how to quantify value.*

During my 19 years as a business consultant helping clients increase profits, I've found that this is the single greatest challenge they face in increasing revenues. The inability to quantify value makes it impossible to communicate that value. This, in turn, leaves customers with the impossible task of trying to decide which offering really has the greatest value.

As a CPA, I've been taught to quantify all sorts of things, including the value that client offerings have for their customers. Once my clients understand how to quantify value, they have no problem communicating that value and distinguishing their offerings from those of their competitors.

Pricing for Profit provides the tools – formulae and sales scripts, as well as an understanding of buyer and seller psychology – to help you command and get higher prices. These tools will give you the confidence you need to stand firm on your price.

Confidence comes from knowledge. When you *know* how to quantify and communicate the value of your offerings, when you *know* that you're charging a fair price, when you *know* how to bundle offerings to meet a variety of budgets, you'll have the confidence you need to:

- Attract customers who value what you provide.
- Gracefully walk away from prospects who don't.
- Avoid the scarcity mentality that plagues many business owners.

The goal of *Pricing for Profit* is to help you get compensated well for the value you provide. In subsequent chapters, I'll share the approaches that I've used to help my clients raise prices *and* increase the number of customers they serve.

While that may seem improbable or even impossible, the reality is that when you can quantify and clearly communicate the value your offerings provide, buyers feel more comfortable buying from you. That's how you attract more customers while charging higher prices. That's how you overcome the fear of losing sales.

My consultant friends jokingly label me "the leading cause of inflation" because I help so many business owners raise their prices. The reality is that I'm simply helping my clients get compensated well for the value they provide. What isn't so obvious is that I'm also helping their customers and prospects make better buying decisions.

Buyers equipped with a clear understanding of value make better buying decisions. They are *not* as easily swayed by emotional arguments because they have facts. They are also not as likely to postpone decisions. Often, we can trace buyer inertia to their uncertainty about the value they'll receive. Poor decisions and no decision are costly to both you and your customers. How expensive can this be?

In Chapter 1, you'll discover:

- How low prices created the subprime debacle and how costly it is for consumers.
- The hidden costs associated with attracting a WalMart store.
- How costly American Airlines flight cancellations were to passengers.

Once you get a sense for how costly low prices can be in Chapter 1, subsequent chapters will provide answers to such questions as:

- Why can't my salespeople sell value the way I do?
- How do I attract more of the right customers?

- How do I generate more dollars on each sale?
- How can I improve my sales close rate?
- How do I price in a down economy?
- How do I make more money without working harder?

Not only will I provide the answers to these questions, *I promise that the answers will be simple, easy to implement, and inexpensive.* Here's the kind of result you can expect:

After only six hours of coaching, a horse trainer learned how to bundle her offerings and communicate their value. In doing so, she was able to increase the price of her core offering 33 percent. Within 60 days she went from a 95 percent vacancy rate to 5 percent.

How was she able to effect such a dramatic turnaround? She knew how to communicate value to her customers and prospects. Her knowledge, and the confidence it afforded, instilled confidence in her customers and prospects, making it easier for them to buy from her.

Another client's change-order revenue losses were eliminated with a two-paragraph memo. Not only did the memo increase revenues, it reduced the age of their accounts receivable by 15 days, freeing up more than $350,000 in cash.

Free yourself of the chains of competitors' pricing. It's time to be compensated well for the tremendous value you provide. Develop the confidence you need to command and get higher prices so that you and your customers can avoid *the high cost of low prices.*

Ignorance Isn't Bliss:
It's EXPENSIVE

Every business owner I've met has been able to tell me exactly why his offerings are better than his competitors'. Yet, when I ask how he prices his offerings, he's almost always *at or below* market. Why this incongruity? Here are some of the more common reasons I'm given:

- We don't have the name awareness of the big boys.
- Our customers only care about price.
- Our competitors won't raise prices, so we can't.
- We'll lose sales (market share).

As you'll see later in this chapter, these "reasons" are smoke and mirrors. They mask the real reason why business owners don't charge higher prices – *they don't know how to convert value into dollars and cents.*

Unless you've entered business from an accounting or finance background, you are probably experiencing the same problem. You simply haven't been trained to make these conversions. We're going to remedy that in Chapter 3. Before we do, let's take a look at how costly this lack of knowledge can be.

Costly for You

First, let's look at lost revenues and their impact on your bottom line. Then we'll look at some less obvious costs.

Lost Revenues: Leaving Money on the Table
This section will give you a sense for how much money you're leaving on the table because you don't have the tools to quantify value. We're going

to begin with some illustrative price increases to demonstrate the magnitude of the dollars available to you through price increases. In Chapter 3, we'll get into the specific formulae you need to determine what price increases you can effect for the products and services you offer. For now, I simply want you to get a sense of the dollars you're foregoing. Let's begin with a very small increase.

What would a 1 percent price increase do for you? There aren't any additional production costs or overhead costs associated with a price increase. Although you have to pay additional income taxes, the rest of the price increase falls to your bottom line. How much is that? Here's the formula for a 1 percent price increase:

$$(1\% \times revenues) - (revenue\ increase \times income\ tax\ rate)$$
$$= bottom\ line\ improvement$$

Table 1-1 shows what a 1 percent increase would do for the bottom line of three different size companies (state income taxes have been ignored for these calculations because the rates vary from state to state and some states do not have corporate income taxes).

Before you begin dreaming about how you'd use that extra money, let's do the same calculations for 3 percent, 5 percent, and 10 percent price increases. Table 1-2 shows the results you could expect from each of these price increases.

When you performed the 10 percent calculation, did you experience some queasiness? Was your heart was beating a little faster? Did you have visions of your customers racing to your competitors? That's

Table 1-1. Bottom Line Potential from a 1 % Price Increase

Current Revenues	$1 million	$10 million	$100 million
1% increase	$10,000	$100,000	$1,000,000
Federal corporate income tax rate	35%	35%	35%
Income tax	$3,500	$35,000	$350,000
Profit gained from a 1% price increase	$6,500	$65,000	$650,000

Table 1-2. Bottom Line Potential for 3%, 5% and 10% Price Increases

Current Revenues	$1 million	$10 million	$100 million
After tax profit from a 3% price increase	$19,500	$195,000	$1,950,000
After tax profit from a 5% increase	$32,500	$325,000	$3,250,000
After tax profit from a 10% increase	$65,000	$650,000	$6,500,000

natural. The reality is that a 10 percent higher price has little impact on a committed buyer. Here are some examples that demonstrate why I can make that statement with such confidence.

Let's say that you're a car aficionado and you really like the Lexus. How much more will you pay for that Lexus over a Camry? A Lexus sedan starts at $31,155; the Camry sedan is $19,145. The price of the Lexus is 62 percent higher than the Camry. That's a lot more than the 10 percent we've been talking about.

You're probably thinking, "That's fine for people who can afford the Lexus, but not everyone can." You're right – to a degree. People have to be able to afford what they're buying, but they'll find a way to afford what they want. I'm sure that you've driven by an old, weathered, and shabby mobile home only to be surprised by the presence of a brand new $30,000 pickup truck in the driveway. You've seen 50-year-old, 900-square-foot houses with a $100,000+ recreational vehicle parked in front. These are examples of people paying premiums for what they truly want, and those premiums are well beyond the 10 percent cited in the examples above.

What are you willing to pay a premium to get? Let's say that you want a new sweater. Where are you going to shop? JCPenney, where you'll get an attractive, serviceable sweater for a modest price? Macy's, where you can get a designer brand, but will pay about twice the price of the JCPenney sweater? Nordstrom's, with its incredible ambience and exceptional personal service, where you'll pay four to six times (yes, that's 400 percent to 600 percent) more for your sweater than you would at

JCPenney? It depends on what you want – on how important image and service are to you.

You've got your new sweater and you're dying to show it off when a friend calls wanting to meet for a drink. "What'll you have?," asks the bartender. Indeed, what will you have? You order Jack Daniels' bourbon. Did you know that Jack Daniels' bourbon whiskeys range in price from $18.98 to $49.99 for a 750 ml bottle? The highest price is almost three times the lowest price offering.

The point is that people make trade-offs in their spending. They'll pay as little as possible for things they need, but don't want. Conversely, they'll pay extraordinary premiums for things they want, but don't need. As you've seen, these premiums can be as high as 600 percent. Actually, they're higher if you're a technology junkie.

People who simply must have the latest and greatest technology will pay as much as 12 times (1,200 percent) what they'd pay when market saturation has been achieved. If you doubt that, look at the history of VCR and DVD players. When they first came out, they were priced around $1,200; that's for a player with no recording capability. When virtually every household in America had multiple players, the price dropped to less than $100.

Have I convinced you that people will pay huge premiums for what they really want? My guess is that, while you can acknowledge the premiums we've just discussed, you can't quite see your offerings in those categories. We'll deal with that issue later in this chapter. Right now, we're considering the high cost of low prices to you, and we've only scratched the surface.

So far we've determined how much revenue and bottom line loss you experience by foregoing a 1 percent to 10 percent price increase (Tables 1-1 and 1-2). Here are some of the less obvious costs.

Productivity Costs

McKinsey & Company, an international consulting firm, published a study entitled *The War for Talent*.[1] McKinsey's research showed that an "A" player typically costs a company 20 percent more in direct compensation than a "B" player. The "A" players, however, produce two to three times as much as a "B" player. That's a 100 percent to 200 percent increase in productivity. What implications does that have?

Think of productivity in terms of revenue capacity. How much more revenue could you generate if you could afford all "A" players on your team? Theoretically, 200 percent to 300 percent. If you're currently generating $1 million in revenues, your sales could grow to $3 million without having to add staff.

Of course, it isn't realistic to think that everyone in your organization is going to be an "A" player. So let's take a more realistic view. Let's see how much your revenue capacity and profits would increase if you could replace 10 percent of your work force with "A" players.

Let's use the same three income levels ($1 million, $10 million, and $100 million) from our earlier examples to help us visualize what lost productivity costs us. Here's the logic behind the math we'll be using.

We're going to assume that we're only going to get the increased productivity from the new "A" players – the new 10 percent of your work force. We're going to assume that they have no impact at all on their coworkers' productivity. That's an unrealistic assumption because "A" players raise the bar, making it necessary for all other players to elevate their performance as well. It is, however, a conservative assumption, which means that you can expect even better results than those calculated below.

We're also going to assume that your labor costs prior to hiring the "A" players is 25 percent of your total revenues. We're going to use the study's statistics and say that the "A" players are going to cost 20 percent more and that they'll produce 100 percent more (the low end of the range cited). Finally, we're going to assume that labor has been the limiting factor in growing sales – that demand exists for your offerings.

Table 1-3 shows the increased revenue and bottom line benefit you could expect by replacing just 10 percent of your work force with "A" players.

As you can see, there are significant profits to be gained from having the money to hire the best and brightest for your organization. How do you get the money? By charging prices that compensate you for the value you provide. I do not believe in gouging the customer, but most businesspeople err on the side of giving the customer much more value than the price they're paying would warrant. We want to narrow that gap. The price you charge must always be less than the value you provide. If the customer isn't going to gain anything from making a purchase, she doesn't have a reason to buy.

Table 1-3. Bottom Line Impact from "A" Players

Current Revenues	$1 million	$10 million	$100 million
10% of revenues (portion associated with work force being replaced)	$100,000	$1,000,000	$10,000,000
Increased revenue potential (previous line × 100%)	$100,000	$1,000,000	$10,000,000
Labor costs prior to adding "A" players (current revenues × 25% current labor cost)	$250,000	$2,500,000	$25,000,000
Additional labor costs (previous line × 10% of work force replaced with "A" players × 20% higher wage cost)	$5,000	$50,000	$500,000
Additional pretax profits (increased revenues less additional labor costs)	$95,000	$950,000	$9,500,000
Federal corporate income tax rate	35%	35%	35%
Federal income tax	$33,250	$332.500	$3,325,000
Increase in after tax profits from having 10% of work force staffed with "A" players)	$61,750	$617,500	$6,175,000

This is still only part of the story, though. There's more to be gained. Let's see how much you can add to your bottom line by ridding yourself of those customers who drive you nuts – the ones who don't value what you offer.

Wrong Customers

There is a variation of Pareto's principle (the 80/20 rule) that says 80 percent of your customers produce 120 percent of your profits. The other 20 percent cost you money. Why does this happen? Why do we hang on to customers who cost us money?

Many accounting systems, especially in small to mid-sized businesses, are not designed to measure profitability by customer. This leaves you, the business owner, with the ill-conceived measure "average profit per customer." Averages mask the fact that some of your customers (all too often, those who account for the greatest portion of your revenues) are costing you money. If you're one of these business owners, set this book aside. Walk to your finance person's office. Instruct him or her to make a customer-profitability tracking system the number one priority. Then resume reading.

Lack of information regarding customer profitability, combined with the perceived constraint of "industry" pricing, creates a scarcity mentality in business owners. The fear of not being able to replace lost revenues causes many business owners to continue their unsuccessful attempts to satisfy customers who simply can't be satisfied.

How much does this fear cost you? Based on the Pareto variation mentioned above, 20 percent of your profits. Table 1-4 gives us a sense for how expensive that can be. The only assumption in this example is that your *pretax* profit is 12 percent of revenues.

Table 1-4. Bottom Line Impact of Firing Unprofitable Customers

Current Revenues	$1 million	$10 million	$100 million
Pretax profits at 12% of revenues	$120,000	$1,200,000	$12,000.000
20% of profits lost on unprofitable customers	$24,000	$240,000	$2,400,000
Federal corporate income tax rate	35%	35%	35%
Federal income tax on additional profits	$8,400	$84,000	$840,000
After tax profits	$15,600	$156,000	$1,560,000

These are the kinds of profit increases you could experience by walking away from the customers from hell—the ones who don't value what you offer, who are never pleased with the deal they got, and who constantly waste huge chunks of your and your staff's time trying to appease them. I'd like to reiterate that the reasons why you're not walking away is that (1) you feel locked into industry pricing and (2) you "know" what it takes to replace business, even bad business, so you stay with customers that you should be cutting loose.

We're not finished yet! Let's not forget that ridding yourself of the wrong customers frees 20 percent of your capacity. If you replace that 20 percent with your ideal customers, those who value what you offer, you can add even more to your bottom line. Table 1-5 gives us a sense for how much. For purposes of this example, I assumed that your new customers value your offerings and that they, like your good customers, are paying the 10 percent price premium suggested earlier.

If we combine the profit potential from Table 1-4 (eliminating unprofitable customers) with the profits potential of Table 1-5 (replacing unprofitable customers), we get a true sense for how costly the wrong customers are. The math has been done for you in Table 1-6.

You've added almost 3 percent (2.86 percent) to your bottom line; that's 37 percent more than you were earning previously. How did I arrive at that? I used our earlier assumptions of 12 percent *pretax* profits and a 35 percent Federal corporate tax rate and performed the following calculation:

Table 1-5. Bottom Line Impact of Replacing Unprofitable Customers

Current Revenues	$1 million	$10 million	$100 million
Revenue replacement (20% of current revenues)	$200,000	$2,000,000	$20,000.000
10% price increase	$20,000	$200,000	$2,000,000
Federal corporate income tax rate	35%	35%	35%
Federal income tax	$7,000	$70,000	$700,000
Profit gained from replacement customers paying 10% price increase	$13,000	$130,000	$1,300,00

Table 1-6. Profit Potential of Replacing Wrong Customers

Current Revenues	$1 million	$10 million	$100 million
Table 1-4 after tax profit	$15,600	$156,000	$1,560,000
Table 1-5 after tax profits	$13,000	$130,000	$1,300,000
Profits from replacing wrong customers	$28,600	$286,000	$2,860,000

Before replacing wrong customers:

Pretax profit (as % of revenue)	12.0%
Federal corporate tax (12% × 35%)	4.2%
After tax profit (as % of revenue)	7.8%
Additional profit from replacing wrong customers	2.9%
Percentage improvement (2.9%/7.8%)	37%

By replacing the wrong customers with people who value your offerings you increase your "take home" pay by 37% percent 2.9 percent divided by 7.8 percent. We're not finished yet. There are more hidden costs.

Other Hidden Costs

Here are some of the more common costs companies incur and the reasons why they incur them:

- Interest costs (easy payment terms).
- Delivery costs (quick turnaround).
- Staffing costs (additional services).
- Quality (distinguishing your offerings).

All of these, and many more, are absorbed by your company in its efforts to distinguish your offerings from your competitors'. Why? Your price isn't doing that job for you; it's the same price everyone else is using.

I won't calculate these costs here, because they vary so widely from industry to industry. Instead, I'm going to provide you with the formulae for performing the calculations yourself.

Interest Costs

If you're providing favorable payment terms, the average age of your accounts receivable is going up. To determine how costly this is:

1. Calculate your average days' sales (annual revenue/365 days or annual revenue/264 days, if you're only open Monday through Friday).
2. Multiply the solution in #1 by the number of additional days you allow your customers' on their payment terms. This is the dollar amount of additional accounts receivable that you're carrying.
3. Multiply #2 by the interest rate on your line of credit or whatever financing source you're using. If your cash flows are adequate to fund these receivables without borrowing money, use the interest rate that you could get from investing this cash in money market accounts, savings accounts, or short-term CDs. This is what your favorable payment terms are costing you. Are they being recouped in your pricing?

If your claim to fame is that you're much more responsive than your competitors - that you provide quicker turnaround - how often do you incur extra delivery costs because the system fails and you have to overnight or special deliver to your customers? What do these system failures cost you? Here's an easy approach to calculating that cost:

1. For a one-month period, track every special delivery you make, how much it cost you, and how much you recouped from the customer. Total the unrecovered costs. This total will tell you what cost you incurred during the month by using quick turnaround time as your competitive advantage.
2. Calculate the total number of orders on which you ate these delivery costs.
3. Divide that number by the total number of orders for the month. This tells you what percentage of your orders are costing you money.
4. Multiply the percentage from #3 by the total number of deliveries you make in a year to get a sense for what your annual costs are.

5. Take the total dollar amount of delivery costs you ate during the month and divide by the number of orders on which you incurred those costs. This gives you an average cost per order.
6. Multiply the average cost per order in #5 by the solution to #4, the estimated total number of orders per year on which you absorb delivery costs. This is how much your quick turnaround time strategy is costing you.

Staffing Costs

When you provide additional services, whether it's phone support, free installation, or a myriad of other services, you have to add staff. The question is, "What does it cost to provide these services?" Here's one way of answering that question:

1. Calculate the number of people it takes to provide these services; it's okay to have fractions, as some people split their time between other duties and these additional service offerings.
2. Calculate the annual rate of pay for these individuals (to make the math simple, I typically multiply their hourly rate by 2,000 hours).
3. Divide your total benefit package costs by your total labor dollars to determine what percentage your benefit costs are to labor dollars; don't forget to include your matching social security costs, worker's compensation insurance, and similar costs, along with the health care and retirement plan costs
4. Multiple the annual pay calculated in #2 above by 1 plus the percentage from #3 (if your benefit cost is 20 percent, multiply by 1.2 to get the combined labor and benefit costs). This is what you're paying for providing these additional services.

Quality Costs

A printer taught me this lesson very early in my career. He asked me whether I thought that his customers wanted a good print job or a great print job. "Great print job!," I said. He gave me one of those gotcha' grins and said, "Most people can't tell the difference between a good print job and a great print job. Plus a great print job is very expensive. My customers want a good print job."

Are there aspects of quality that you've built into your offerings that your customers don't value – that they wouldn't be willing to pay extra to get? If so, here's how you can calculate the cost:

1. Determine what equipment is involved in adding the quality. Then calculate the acquisition and operating costs associated with that equipment. Acquisition cost is the purchase price of the equipment plus installation costs and financing costs over the life of the equipment. Operating costs include regular maintenance, major overhauls, utility costs, insurance, and so on.
2. Convert the acquisition cost to an hourly cost by dividing the total acquisition cost by the anticipated hours of life the equipment has. Equipment lives are typically stated in some measure of time—such as years or hours of operation—that make it easy to determine the number of hours of you can expect from the equipment.
3. Convert the equipment operating costs to an hourly cost.
4. Use the staffing cost formula above to calculate the hourly rate your employees are spending on quality development (design), production, and assurance (testing).
5. Add the hourly rates for equipment acquisition cost, equipment operating costs, and staffing costs.
6. Multiply #5 by the number of hours of operation of the equipment. This will give you a reasonable estimate of the cost of quality you're incurring, but not recovering, in your pricing.

Once you've calculated these hidden costs, you can add them to the results in Table 1-7, which shows the bottom line benefit that can be gained by:

1. Increasing prices by 10 percent.
2. Replacing 10 percent of your work force with "A" players.
3. Replacing the wrong customers with those who value your offerings.

As you can see, we're simply summarizing the data from earlier tables.

Table 1-7. Total Profit Improvement Potential

	$1 million	*$10 million*	*$100 million*
Profits from a 10% price increase (Table 1-2)	$65,000	$650,000	$6,500,000
Profit from "A" player productivity (Table 1-3)	$61,750	$617,500	$6,175,000
Profits from replacing wrong customers with ideal customers (Table 1-6)	$28,600	$286,000	$2,860,000
Total profit improvement	$155,350	$1,553,500	$15,535,000
profit improvement as a % of revenues	15.5%	15.5%	15.5%

That's right! Given even the modest assumptions we've made in the exercises above, you would gain 15.5 percent more of every revenue dollar falling to your bottom line. That's huge. How would you use the money? Increase your competitive advantage? Diversify your portfolio? Spend more time with your family?

Now that you have a sense of the payback that raising prices can have for you and your organization, let's deal with that nagging fear that's still hanging out there – the fear of losing revenues. Here's an extreme example, referred to earlier, of what can occur when you learn how to price and bundle your offerings more effectively.

A horse trainer was referred to me by a client. When she finally got around to calling, she had a 95 percent vacancy rate in her barn. Despite providing incredible service, she was charging *below-market* rates. She was taking a double hit to her bottom line. Her costs were higher than her competitors' because she was providing higher levels of service. Her revenues were lower because she was charging below-market prices.

We raised the price of her core offering – the boarding service – by 33 percent, making it 10 percent higher than the market. We also bundled the boarding with training and show services and developed her sales script to help customers understand the value they were getting. Within 60 days, her vacancy went from 95 percent to 5 percent. She picked up 25 new weekly riding lessons and had so many horses for a show that she had to build temporary stalls.

How can this be? How could she raise prices by 33 percent and generate more business? She was able to convert the value she was providing into dollars and cents and communicate that monetary value to her customers. Customers pay for value when they understand what that value is. They, like you, haven't been trained to make those calculations.

You and your company aren't the only ones to suffer from low prices. Your customers do as well. How? Let's take a look.

Costly for Your Customers

The high cost of low prices isn't always obvious. Here are some of the ways consumers pay dearly for low prices, often without knowing it. By the way, let's not forget that we, too, are consumers who are paying these costs.

Subprime Mortgages

The U.S. Congress just passed a $787 billion stimulus package. This is on top of an $85 billion dollar bailout of American International Group (AIG), a global insurer of financial instruments to the banking and finance industry, as well as the estimated $25 billion cost of the government take over of Fannie Mae and Freddie Mac. Nor does it include $13 billion lent to General Motors and Chrysler or the projected $275 billion housing bailout plan. That's $1.185 trillion of costs that don't take into consideration the stock market hit (more than $8.4 trillion dollars over a seven-day period in 2008).[2]

Yes, I know that lax underwriting standards, inflated appraisals, failed regulatory oversight, and Wall Street greed contributed to this problem, but do you think that these home buyers would have applied for loans if the price of money hadn't been so cheap? I doubt it. The vast majority of people don't want to risk their credit standings, their personal and retirement assets, or their good names by buying things they can't afford.

What, then, caused them to take the risks they did? Cheap mortgage money. Low interest rates reduce monthly payments. Lower payments allow buyers to purchase more house than they can typically afford. Buyers, recognizing the opportunity, rush to buy larger homes while they can afford them. In doing so, they drive up the price of the homes.

As sellers experience higher profits on their home sales, they begin to view homes as a great investment vehicle instead of as a place to live that has some upside potential. This change in attitude, coupled with an extended period of low interest rates and the high profits they triggered, cause homeowners to become real estate "investors." Soon, people were "flipping" homes – buying and selling them in a matter of months – to garner previously unheard of profits. The result is the subprime disaster that plagues the global economy.

The numbers are so huge that few, if any of us, can wrap our minds around them. Let's see if we can make these numbers more relevant. There are approximately 304 million people in the United States, according to the Census Bureau projections.[3] The $1.2 trillion in bailouts and $8.4 trillion stock market hit total $9.6 trillion dollars. That's $31,579 for every man, woman, and child in the United States.

The full impact of these losses may never be known. One thing is certain, though; they'll be borne by us as consumers. They'll appear in the form of higher taxes, more government regulation, and higher prices (some related to the higher cost of regulatory compliance; some resulting from inflation).

Isn't that interesting? We're going to pay higher prices in the future because we didn't pay them previously. Abnormally low prices, such as those experienced in the mortgage market, only postpone price increases. They don't eliminate them. Unfortunately, price increases, when postponed for extended periods of time, grow exponentially. We thus find ourselves paying much more than we would have if pricing had reflected true value.

Let's see what costs we incur when one of the world's most popular retailers enters the market. Yes, I'm speaking of WalMart.

WalMart

Whenever I counsel business owners against using a low-price strategy, I inevitably hear "But what about WalMart?" Indeed, WalMart is a huge success story and its success, to date, has been based on a low-price strategy. This isn't the whole story.

WalMart's success reflects a tireless commitment to cutting costs, which is something most business owners don't enjoy. In fact, when I ask business owners in my pricing and finance seminars and college finance classes, "How many of you awaken in the morning thinking 'Wow, I get to cut costs today!,'" no one raises their hand. None of them has a passion for cutting costs. Yet, that's been one of the keys to WalMart's success in implementing its low-price strategy. Their management has a passion for doing what others abhor.

Unfortunately, those of us who buy from WalMart don't have a clear picture of the true cost we're paying. Many communities, in order to attract a WalMart store, have had to revamp their road systems and enhance their infrastructures *at taxpayer expense.*

Employee and labor department lawsuits against WalMart dealing with everything from discrimination, use of illegal aliens, and having employees work "off the clock" indicate that members of our community are paying a price in terms of employment and earnings. Some of these practices result in fewer workers being employed. Others limit employees' income, which means they have fewer dollars to spend. Fewer jobs and lower earnings reduce discretionary income, which in turn reduces demand for non-WalMart products and services. This limits the number of jobs and salary levels available to employees in businesses not serving WalMart. In essence, these practices serve to slow economic growth.

A similar effect is experienced by vendors serving WalMart. Many are not adept at cost cutting and have, consequently, been "eating" the price reductions required to keep their WalMart vendor status. Diminished profits in these vendor firms inevitably translate into lower business investment and slower job growth. I'm not blaming WalMart for its suppliers' inability to control costs, but the effect is there nonetheless.

It's not my intent to bash WalMart. It, like all firms employing a low-price strategy, finds it increasingly difficult to lower costs to maintain its low-price leadership. As costs approach the floor (the point at which costs can no longer fall, but must rise), they begin to push the envelope. That's when we see the abuses that lead to lawsuits and community action like WalMart is experiencing.

To its credit, WalMart's leadership has recognized that it has reached the floor. The most obvious evidence of this is the change in its tagline from, "Always low prices, always" to "Save money. Live Better." If WalMart is successful in making the transition, some of the hidden costs we've discussed will be converted to higher prices, which is where they should have been all along. Had these hidden costs been known, it's likely that we, as consumers, would have made some different buying decisions.

American Airlines

On April 8th and 9th, 2008, American Airlines cancelled more than 1,500 flights, stranding roughly 150,000 passengers, because of wiring harness problems in its MD-80 planes. American paid a heavy price in lost revenues, but it was not the only one to have suffered losses.

Companies whose employees were on those flights suffered lost revenues as well as productivity losses. To get a sense for how costly this was, simply take your average sales per day and multiple it by the number of salespeople you have traveling. That's what it would have cost you if all of your salespeople were scheduled to travel via American Airlines that day. Add to that the number of production people in your organization who weren't able to get to the customers they were supposed to serve. How many billable hours did that represent? You can't recover those billing days, so the revenue potential for those days was completely lost.

Passengers who were vacationing lost those vacation days – a heavy price given that Americans typically don't use all of their vacation time. Imagine having your employees returning tired, frustrated, and still exhausted from an extended period without a vacation. What is that going to do to their productivity in the next six months to a year? Will their productivity drop 10 percent, 20 percent, more? What about the lost productivity when they weren't able to report back to work on time?

For those hoping to visit family and friends, the time lost is irreplaceable. Imagine that you were scheduled to visit your grandkids and these were the last two vacation days you had available to make this trip. There isn't enough money in the world to compensate you for the loss of time with your grandchildren.

The "Big Three" Automakers

I want to include this example because it demonstrates a common mistake made with pricing. For decades, GM, Ford, and Chrysler have taught us to wait for a deal. Wait for 0 percent financing, wait for rebates, wait for both 0 percent financing *and* a rebate, wait for employee pricing. They have, in essence, trained us to not to buy from them unless we get a deal.

So what's the problem? They've dug a deep hole for themselves. Instead of dealing with the labor issues, the lack of inspiring designs, quality control issues, and fuel efficiency issues they've faced for decades, they've chosen to use low prices to accelerate future sales into current periods.

As of this writing, these automakers had asked the Federal government for $50 billion in loans to help them develop the technology for alternative fuels. In the face of Congressional dismay, they quickly reduced the request to $25 billion. As mentioned earlier, General Motors and Chrysler received $13 billion in 2008 and are seeking another $21 billion. To make matters worse, those of us whose retirement plans include investment in GM and Ford stock have seen the value of our investment decline by more than 50 percent in the past 5 years.[4] These costs certainly weren't reflected in the sticker price of the automobiles we bought.

As you can see, many costs we don't see are directly related to low prices. Costs that, had we been aware of them, could have altered our buying decisions – could have helped us make more informed decisions.

Now that we've had an opportunity to see how expensive low prices can be for us and our customers, let's revisit those "reasons" for not raising prices outlined at the beginning of the chapter. They're listed below for your convenience.

"Reasons" for Not Raising Prices

The most common reasons for not raising prices are:

- We don't have the name awareness of the big boys.
- Our customers only care about price.
- Our competitors won't raise prices, so we can't.
- We'll lose sales (market share).

As I mentioned earlier, these reasons are just smoke and mirrors clouding the real issue – the fact that we don't know how to calculate the monetary value of the intrinsic value our offerings provide. Let's begin with name awareness or the lack thereof.

Our Lack of Name Awareness

A residential homebuilder client told me that he couldn't raise prices because he didn't have the name awareness of the big builders. This, after he'd just spent 45 minutes telling me why his quality was better than "the big boys."

Upon hearing this, I asked him if he advertised in the local paper. He did. Then I asked him to envision that he and two of the top builders in town all had subdivisions in the same area, with similar size homes and elevations (styles) and that they all advertised on the same page in the real estate section of the paper. The only difference between his homes and those of his competitors was that his price was 10 percent lower. What would he, as a buyer, think upon seeing that ad?

"I'd think that the low-price builder was cutting corners!" he replied. Indeed, the message his pricing was sending was exactly the opposite of what he believed. *He believed that his product was better, but his pricing indicated that it was inferior.*

Pricing is not the tool to use to create name awareness. That's what your marketing messages should be doing. Marketing is the tool for shouting your competitive advantage – an advantage that people value and are willing to pay premium prices to get. We're talking about the advantages that Lexus has over Camry; Nordstrom has over JCPenney; Jack Daniels' single barrel bourbon whiskey has over its Old No. 7 brand.

A Lesson from Retailers

If you feel that you absolutely must lower your price to get in the door, take a lesson from retailers. Preface your offer with "This time only. . . ." There are times when a prospect is happy with his or her current vendor and doesn't want to change. The only way that you're going to get a shot at that business is to offer an incentive to try your offerings. That's when you make it clear that you're extending a one-time offer.

Language that works well for me, and my clients, is:

> *"I know that you're happy with your current vendor, and you need a reason to give me a try, so I'm going to extend this offer only on the first order. (State the offer.) I'm sure that you're going to be so delighted with our (quality, service, speed) that you want to use us again and again."*

This approach is especially helpful for those of you who have recently gone into business and are trying to land that first customer/client.

Buyers appreciate the business acumen you demonstrate in acknowledging the fact that they're "taking a risk" by going with a vendor with a limited track record. They appreciate being compensated for taking that risk. Add these factors to the confidence demonstrated by your statement, "I'm sure that you're going to be so delighted . . . ," and you'll find that your odds of closing the sale go up dramatically.

A Final Point on Name Awareness

Whenever you feel tempted to lower your price because you don't have a well-established reputation, ask yourself the following question: Would I rather have the prospect walk away saying "I wish I could afford his offerings" or "His price is low; I wonder if his offerings are any good?"

Remember that name awareness is the goal of marketing, not pricing. Your price should reflect the value you provide. That brings us to the second reason for not raising prices: customers' sole focus on price.

Our Customers Only Care About Price

Did I mention "The Big Three" automakers? Do you think that they might have felt that way? Was it true? Of course not! People have been buying Toyotas and Hondas even though they are priced higher than their GM, Ford, and Chrysler counterparts. Why? Because buyers value other aspects of the offerings more than they value low prices.

In the case of Toyota and Honda, buyers value the reliability and convenience that their cars engender over a lower price. Buyers understand that besides spending $1,000 to repair their American-made cars at 50,000 miles, they'd have to jockey schedules to make sure the kids got to school on time, that the car got to the shop before work, that Mom and Dad got to work on time, that the kids got to band or soccer practice in the evening, and that the car got picked up before the repair shop closed. These are some of the reasons why people have paid higher prices for Toyotas and Hondas.

Another reason business owners think that buyers only care about price is that buyers bring up the subject so early in the discussion. Why do buyers do that? In many cases it's because they can't tell the difference between your offerings and your competitors'. Couple this lack of differentiation with their inability to quantify value (remember, you're not the only one suffering from this malady), and price becomes the only yardstick by which they feel they can measure it.

If it appears that your customers only care about price, revisit your sales and marketing messages. You're probably not doing a very good job of communicating the advantages your offerings provide or reflecting that in the prices you charge.

Our Competitors Won't Raise Prices

Of course not! Their offerings are inferior to yours. My clients know when that's true, and you do as well.

This, the third reason for not raising prices, doesn't hold water if your products and services are, indeed, better than your competitors', *and* your customers value the difference. You should get compensated for that value regardless of whether your competitors are willing to raise prices. People expect to pay more to get more, but only if it has value to them.

Your ability to get higher prices than your competitors lies squarely on your ability to demonstrate greater value and to monetize that value for the customer. If you can do that, you can get higher pricing. It won't matter that your competitors refuse to raise their prices. If you're still skeptical, let's look at a fairly common occurrence. You've probably done this yourself.

You drive a greater distance *and* pay a slightly higher price for what you want because the people are friendlier or they'd previously gone above and beyond the call of duty to help you with a problem. Whatever the reason, you paid extra in the forms of drive time and cash to get the experience you wanted. The fact that their competitors were closer and had lower prices didn't prevent you from spending more.

Now for our final "reason" for not raising prices– we'll lose market share.

We'll Lose Market Share

Unfortunately, the financial press often speaks of market share as if all customers are equally valuable. As we saw in our discussion of the wrong customers above, there are tremendous costs involved in dealing with people who don't value what you offer.

The first thing to understand about market share is that there are a limited number of people (it could be a large number, but it is a finite number) who value what you provide. Market share should be calculated in light of this number, and not, as is often done, in light of the total number of buyers who *might* use your product or service. Why use the smaller number?

Let's say that your market, the people who will pay significantly more for your offering because they value what you provide, is 100,000 buyers. Let's further assume that you've saturated your market, which, to me, means that you've achieved about 70 percent market share (70,000 customers from this group).

Some of you are wondering "Why 70 percent?" I don't have any hard data, but most of us abhor a monopoly. We understand that monopolies put us at the mercy of the seller. To avoid that, we begin shifting our business to other companies when we feel that one company is gaining too much market share. We're going to err on the side of shifting business early in case others don't see the trend as quickly as we do. That, I believe, occurs around 70 percent market saturation. I know I'm dating myself with this example, but monopoly avoidance is one of the reasons that, in the early days of the Internet, people used Netscape instead of the Microsoft browser. They wanted a choice. Hopefully, this minor digression will help make this example more relevant for you.

In this example, we're assuming a market of 100,000 buyers with you having a 70 percent market share. You decide to increase "market share" by expanding the market to include people who have an interest in your offering, but who don't really value it enough to pay your price. How do you attract them?

Typically you're going to offer a lower price. It could be in the form of a lower cash price, more favorable payment or delivery terms, or higher quality or additional service. Whatever the form, you have, in essence, lowered your price.

To handle this additional volume, your infrastructure has to grow, with the following results. You will:

1. Spend more to attract these customers, and the sales cycle will become more protracted, thereby driving up both your marketing and sales costs.
2. Invest more in inventory if you're a manufacturer/assembler.
3. Typically experience slower pay because these buyers don't really value what you offer.

4. Pay more interest to finance larger inventories and older receivables.
5. Experience more bad debt losses, because buyers don't value your offerings.
6. Incur more in customer service costs dealing with customer complaints; people who don't value what they buy are easily disappointed.

Attracting that second tier customer is expensive. It's one reason why so many businesses end up with 20 percent of their customers being the wrong customers.

What's the solution? Instead of trying to "expand" your market to disinterested buyers, expand geographically, keeping clearly in mind the profile of your ideal customer or, better yet, identify unsatisfied needs of your existing customer base and fill the gap with new offerings. There are always unsatisfied needs. The company that identifies and fills those needs first can charge whatever it likes because there is no alternative.

As you can see, the four "reasons" for not raising prices have little, if any, validity. In the following chapters, you'll learn how to set aside these excuses and enjoy the compensation you so richly deserve.

Before we get to the methodology for calculating value (Chapter 3), there is something you need to know. Not every seller is capable of demanding and gaining higher prices even when they know how to quantify value. In Chapter 2, we're going to find out why and what you can do if you happen to fall into that category.

Executive Summary

1. There are four "reasons" why business owners don't feel that they can raise prices:
   • We don't have the name awareness of the big boys.
   • Our customers only care about price.
   • Our competitors won't raise prices, so we can't.
   • We'll lose sales (market share).
   None of them are valid.

2. The real reason that business owners don't raise prices is that they don't know how to monetize the intrinsic value of their offerings.

3. The cost of low prices to you, the business owner, is huge. The combined cost of lost revenues, productivity losses, and retaining customers who don't value your offerings can easily reach 15.5 percent of your revenues.

4. Low prices cost your customers, too. The subprime mortgage debacle, which could have been prevented if the price of money hadn't been held artificially low, cost every U.S. citizen at least $31,579. That's a conservative estimate.

5. WalMart, the icon of low prices, is tempering its low-price strategy. Communities, employees, and vendors are no longer willing to bear the high costs of WalMart's low-price strategy.

6. The "Big Three" automakers have taught us to wait for a deal before buying. Are you doing that with your customers?

7. Creating name awareness is the function of your marketing message, not your pricing. Using low prices to "market" your offerings ends up sending the wrong message to the market – a message of poor quality/service.

8. The perception that "customers only care about price" demonstrates the customers' aren't any more adept at monetizing value than you are.

9. "My competitors won't raise prices" is simply an indication that they don't know how to quantify value either. If they could, and their offerings were superior, they would be charging higher prices.

10. The fear of loss of "market share" implies that all customers are equally valuable. The examples above show that the wrong customers can conservatively cost you 1.5 percent on your bottom line (that's after tax dollars). You can double that, 3 percent, if you can replace the wrong customers with those who value your offerings.

CHAPTER 2

Know Thyself . . .
and You'll Know Others, Too

"*Why can't my salespeople sell value the way I do?*" The frustration was etched into the business owner's face. He had tried sales training, mentoring, even going on calls with his salespeople, yet he couldn't get them to sell value.

"What type of buyers are your salespeople?," I asked. His answer was not responsive, so I pressed the question again. "What type of buyers are your salespeople?" "I don't understand your question." he replied. "I don't look at buying habits," he explained. "I focus on their sales records."

He had a completely different perspective once I explained the influence buying habits have on a salesperson's approach to selling.

Selling Styles Mirror Buying Habits

Few businesspeople realize that a person's sales approach is a nearly perfect reflection of his or her buying habits. *There are two types of buyers — price buyers and value buyers.*

Price buyers will tell you that their primary goal is to get the lowest price possible; it's the top consideration in their buying decision. Conversely, value buyers list factors like integrity, quality, dependability, convenience, and the friendliness of the salesperson above price in making their buying decisions. What does this have to do with selling?

Imagine that you are a price buyer and price is the top criteria in making your buying decision. All of the other aspects of the offering pale in importance. Now let's assume that you take a job in sales. When you talk to prospective buyers, what criteria do you expect them to use in making their buying decisions? Price! The same as you do.

Our natural tendency is to assume that we're normal and the rest of the world sees things the way we do. That's why price buyers become price sellers and value buyers become value sellers. Are you a price buyer or value buyer?

Know Thyself

We're going to look at a variety of buying situations. The answers you give will help you determine your natural buying style. The reason I'm using such a broad array of buying situations is that none of us is exclusively a value buyer or price buyer. I'm sure that each of you can point to a purchase and say, "I bought the top of the line." Does that make you a value buyer? Not necessarily.

The opposite is true as well. You have petty economies, things for which you simply refuse to pay full price. Mine happens to be shoes; I'll wait months for a sale to avoid paying full price for shoes. Why? I don't have a clue. It's just the way I'm wired. Let's see how you're wired.

The questions that appear in the sections that follow will help you ascertain whether you are predominantly a price buyer or a value buyer. Take your time. Be honest with yourself. No one will see your answers, so there's no reason to fudge. Besides, the goal of this exercise is to get to know yourself so that you can:

- Employ a business strategy that fits your natural style.
- Determine what types of buyers your customers are and whether they are right for your business.
- Identify quickly a prospect's buying style – price or value.
- Discover whether your salespeople are right for your strategy.
- Determine whether professional managers fit your strategy.

There's a lot at stake here, so let's get this right.

Before we go on, however, let's revisit the definitions of price buyer and value buyer. Unless you and I are using the same definitions, this exercise won't produce the result we desire.

Price buyers are people who view price as their number one criterion in their buying decision. All other aspects of the offering run a distant second to price.

Value buyers view integrity, quality, dependability, friendliness, convenience, ambiance, image, and other aspects of the offering to be more important than price. Value buyers typically place price ninth on the list of criteria considered in their buying decision.[5] Now that we have revisited the definitions, let's begin.

Apparel

What's important to you when buying clothing? Where do you shop?

- Fashion/image/ambiance – Prada, Louis Vuitton, Armani
- Designer clothing/exceptional service/ambiance - Nordstrom, Saks Fifth Avenue
- Designer clothing/limited service/attractive displays - Macy's, Dillard's
- Celebrity and emerging designers/self-serve - JCPenney, Sears, Target
- Price/functionality/self-serve - WalMart, Marshall's, Gordmans

Appliances

What's important to you when you buy appliances? Where do you shop?

- Style/image/ambiance – Specialty stores
- Style/ambiance - Major department stores
- Name brand/knowledgeable sales force - Sears, Lowe's, Home Depot, Best Buy
- Price/functionality - WalMart, Costco

Automobiles

What type of vehicle do you drive? What influences your choice? The list isn't all inclusive, but there's an adequate array for you to determine your buying motivation.

- Head-turning image/luxury - Bentley, Rolls Royce
- Head-turning image/performance – Ferrari, Lamborghini
- Image/luxury - Mercedes, Lexus, Cadillac, Lincoln
- Quality/dependability - Camry, Taurus, Buick
- Functionality/price - Aveo, Focus, Yaris
- Price/functionality - Used cars

Auto Repair

Where do you take your vehicle when you need repairs? Why?

- Manufacturer-trained mechanics/manufacturer parts/ guarantees – Dealers
- Specialized knowledge/skills - Specialty shops (they specialize in certain models, types of cars [i.e. performance cars] or types of repairs – transmissions/cooling)
- Dependable service/after market parts/guarantees/convenience – Automotive repair chains – Sears, regional chains
- Price/service - Local, independent repair shops (I realize that there are some very good independent repair shops, but many of them compete on price)
- Price – Auto parts stores, NAPA, CarQuest, and AutoZone for do-it-yourselfers

Food

Where do you do the bulk of your grocery shopping? Because many food stores are regional chains and their names may not mean anything to you, I'm going to provide descriptions instead of store names.

- Freshness/unusual food items - Specialty stores, farmers' markets, fish markets, meat markets
- Quality/ambiance - Major chains, primarily name brands, a few store brands
- Price - Discount chains, primarily store brands, limited selection, you bag your own groceries

Home Furnishings

Where, and how, do you shop for furniture, draperies, carpeting, and decorations? Again, because there are chains and specialty stores unique to your region, I'm going describe as well as name buying venues.

- Image/uniqueness - Interior designers, art galleries, specialty stores
- Image/attractive designs/high quality – Specialty stores, Macy's, Dillard's
- Quality/reliability/attractive designs - Lowe's, Home Depot, and Sears
- Price/functionality - Outlet stores and discount chains

Electronics

With electronics, it isn't so much where you make your purchase, but when you make it. Some people simply *must* have the latest and greatest even though they may pay as much as ten times the price they'll pay in a year or two.[6] If you're one of these folks, move onto the next question; you're definitely a value buyer. If not, let's consider other factors that can influence your electronics purchase.

- Systems design/installation/service - Custom design stores
- High-end systems/installation - Some custom design stores/ specialty stores
- Quality/name brands/knowledgeable sales force - Best Buy and American TV/Electronics
- Price/functionality/self-serve - WalMart, Kmart, Costco

Business Equipment

What factors influence your business/production equipment purchases?

- Custom designs or modifications/quality/dependability/ performance/reliable repair services - Manufacturers' outlets/ distributors/representatives
- Latest technology/name brands/quality/service – New equipment dealers
- Name brand quality/service - Used equipment dealers
- Price/functionality - auctions, as-is sellers, off-brand dealers (new or used)

Business Supplies

Since this market is dominated primarily by major chain stores—Office Depot, Office Max, and Staples—we're going to look at your attitude toward what you buy as opposed to where you buy?

- Image – supplies *must be* high quality and name brands
- Quality/dependability/guarantee – only use name brand items and manufacturer's replacement parts and supplies
- Price/functionality – store brands, refurbished toner and ink cartridges

Business Services
Again, we're going to look at attitude rather than specific vendors.

- Productivity/quality - you contract with marketing, computer, bookkeeping, finance, tax, human resource, and pricing specialists to do the things you can't do
- Productivity/long-term independence - I hire people to help me develop skills
- Price - I perform clerical tasks rather than hire someone to do them
- Price - I spend more time saving money than generating sales

Are You a Price Buyer or Value Buyer?
Table 2-1 will help you answer the question. Simply mark the column that describes your buying habit for that item, then tally the results.

Do you have more entries in the price buyer column or the value buyer column? If it's a close call or if most of your entries are in the "Neutral Buyer" category, here's another approach you can use. Think of the purchases you *didn't* make; the ones where you simply walked away. Do you have two or three in mind? Now ask yourself "Why did I walk away?" Here are some more questions to help you make that determination:

- Did the offering lack a feature, other than price, that prevented it from meeting my needs?
- Was the salesperson unfriendly or inattentive?
- Did the salesperson offer a solution before identifying my needs?
- Did the salesperson fail to provide information I requested?
- Were my price expectations not met?

Confirmation
Before we go on, let's confirm your assessment by having you talk to three to five people who regularly observe you in buying situations. Here are some questions to ask them; don't be afraid to ask them to cite examples:

- When I'm researching a purchase, where do I focus my attention first: price or the product's advantages and disadvantages?

Table 2-1. Buying Habits

	Price Buyer	Neutral Buyer	Value Buyer
Apparel	WalMart, Marshall's, Gordman's, Target, JCPenney, Sears	Macy's, Dillard's	Nordstrom, Saks Fifth Avenue, Prada, Louis Vuitton, Armani
Appliances	WalMart, Costco	Sears, Lowe's, Home Depot, Best Buy, major department stores	Specialty Stores
Automobiles	Aveo, Focus, Yaris	Camry, Taurus, Buick	Cadillac, Lincoln, Lexus, Mercedes, Lamborghini, Ferrari, Bentley, Rolls Royce
Auto Repair	Do-it-yourselfer, local auto repair shop	Sears, regional auto repair chains	Specialty shops, dealers
Food	Discount chains – primarily store brands, limited selection, bag your own groceries	Major chains – primarily name brands, some store brands, wider selection, baggers	Specialty stores, including farmers', fish, and meat markets

Home Furnishings	Outlet stores and discount chains, Lowe's, Home Depot, Sears	Mid-range specialty stores, Macy's and Dillard's	Interior designers, art galleries and high-end specialty stores
Electronics	WalMart, Costco, Kmart	Best Buy, American	Custom shops and specialty stores
Business Equipment	Off brand, as-is sellers, auctions	Used name-brand equipment	Name-brand manufacturers' outlets, distributors
Business Supplies	Off brands, refurbished toner and ink cartridges	A blend of off brand and name brands – functionality is the focus	Name brands and manufacturers' replacement parts with an eye to image
Business Services	I prefer to do things myself	I hire clerical help, but keep important tasks for myself	I hire professionals and focus on what I do best

- Are brand names important to me, or do I prefer store brands and off brands?
- On a scale of 1 to 5, with 5 being the highest, how important is my image to me?
- Do I typically pay more for quality and dependability?
- Do I regularly go out of my way to get a "great" deal, or do I choose from readily available, reasonable deals?
- Am I more inclined to hire people to do things I can't do for myself or to work through them myself?
- Do I spend more time saving money or making money?

How do their answers compare to yours? Do they have the same perception you do? If not, let's get real. If you're going to choose an effective strategy for your business, you need to know which type of buyer you are.

Before we discuss the relationship between your buying style and your business strategy, let's confirm that your buying habits are, indeed, being reflected in your sales approach. Earlier I said that sales approach is a *nearly perfect* reflection of your buying habits. If you happen to be one of the few for whom that isn't true or you've trained yourself to sell contrary to your nature, let's discover that now by looking at your sales approach.

Sales-Side Confirmation

This time you want to talk with three to five people who regularly observe you in sales situations. Here are the questions to ask:

- In sales calls, do I push price or other aspects of my offerings?
- Do I offer price concessions before they're requested?
- Do I regularly add freebies to sweeten the deal?
- When a prospect asks for a price concession, do I require a concession as well?
- Have you ever seen me tell a prospect, "I don't think we're right for you?"

You're a price buyer if you:

- Tout price over other aspects of your offerings.
- Offer price concessions before they're requested.
- Add freebies to sweeten the deal.

You sell value if you:

- Tout other aspects of your offerings over price.
- Don't give price concessions or freebies without getting a concession.
- Walk away when prospects demand concessions *without* reciprocating.

At this point, you've performed a self-assessment, gained insights from people who've regularly observed you in buying situations, and have had others observe you selling. By now you should have a good sense of whether you are a price buyer/seller or a value buyer/seller.

What do these assessments do for you? They help you determine whether you're using the right business strategy for your nature.

Nature and Strategy

Imagine that you're a *price* buyer/seller trying to differentiate your business on the *value* of its offerings. What do you experience?

- You offer increasingly greater value to attract new customers.
- You offer low prices, often discounting your price before a customer requests a price concession.
- Your production costs go up as you add more value to your offerings.
- Your profit margin suffers – the result of low prices and higher production costs.
- Your overhead increases as unit sales grow, reducing the bottom-line benefit you get from each sales dollar.

Talk about expensive! Increased volume (more work), lower prices (working for less), higher costs (working harder for less). I doubt that's what you envisioned when you started your business.

Now let's shift gears and assume that you're a *value* buyer/seller trying to compete on *price:*

- You enhance your offerings to create greater value as is your nature.

- You don't know how to quantify value so you price at or below industry pricing.
- Your production costs go up as you add value.
- Your profit margin suffers – the result of low prices and higher production costs.
- Your overhead increases as unit sales grow, reducing the bottom-line benefit you get from each sales dollar.

It's the same result! Going against your nature is expensive. What happens when you follow your nature?

Let's assume that you're a natural price buyer/seller. Following your nature, you employ a low-price strategy. WalMart and Southwest Airlines have employed this strategy with great success. You can too, *if* you:

- Are passionate about cost control.
- Realize that price buyers are not loyal; when a competitor offers a lower price, they're gone.
- Understand that there is a limit to how much costs can be cut.
- Recognize that cost cutting encourages shortcuts.
- Realize that you're targeting a limited market.

What impact does each of these have on the success of your low-price strategy?

- A passion for cost control allows you to reduce costs while lowering prices. Neither WalMart nor Southwest gives up all their savings to their customers.
- Disloyal price buyers drive up your marketing costs unless you can maintain low-price leadership.
- There is a limit to how low costs can be driven, as WalMart is discovering through employee lawsuits, vendors saying "No" to further price concessions, and communities voting not to allow WalMart into their boundaries. Southwest hasn't been any more successful than other airlines in negotiating union contracts.[7]
- Heavy cost cutting often results in shortcuts. In March 2008, Southwest paid $10.2 million dollars in fines for flying planes that weren't properly inspected. Not only are fines expensive, but

deferred maintenance always ends up being more expensive than regular maintenance.
- Only 14 percent of the buying public has indicated that price is their number one criterion for buying. That means that 86 percent would be willing to pay a higher price if they only knew the value you provide.[8]

How does this compare with the value buyer/seller using a value strategy? Owners with a value orientation, those who market, sell, and price based on value, can expect:

- A large market; 86 percent of buyers find things like quality, dependability, integrity, convenience, and friendliness more important than price in the buying decision.
- The ability to generate significant revenues on low unit volume sales.
- A smaller investment in production capacity than price sellers.
- Higher margins – the combination of higher prices and lower production capacity.
- Lower infrastructure costs; fewer transactions to be processed than price sellers.
- More of each sales dollar falling to the bottom line.
- Great customer loyalty; value buyers rarely shop when their needs are being met.

In light of the above comparison, would you rather be a low-price buyer using a low-price strategy or a value buyer employing a value strategy? I'll bet that most of you opted for the "work less, make more" value orientation.

If value is your natural style, you won't have any problem adopting and adhering to the concepts laid out in later chapters. That's great news for the value folks, but what do you do if you're price oriented?

First, let me say that I believe that we can train our minds to do anything we want them to do. My program, "7 Steps to Becoming INVALUABLE," teaches people how to overcome the natural tendencies that get in the way of their success. Whether presented in one of my seminars in St. Louis or at association conventions and conferences across the country, members of the audiences see that they do, indeed, have the ability to overcome their natural tendencies. I'm not going to kid you; retraining your mind is hard work. It's an investment of time and energy that you may not want to make. If that's the case, there is an alternative - professional management.

Hire people who have a natural value orientation, hand them this book, then get out of the way. If you don't feel that you can afford professional managers, take another look at the price buyer/price strategy list. If you're experiencing increasing sales volume, shrinking margins, and a rapidly waning bottom line, can you afford *not* to make the change? In the "Know Others, Too" section below, you'll find questions to help you identify and hire professional managers with value buyer/seller mindset.

Now that you have a good sense for what type of buyer/seller you are, let's see how we can use this knowledge to understand others.

Know Others, Too

First, we're going to look at your customers and prospects. How do you know whether they are naturally price buyers or value buyers?

Actually, it's easy. Price buyers want to know the price first. They aren't interested in hearing a lot about your offerings until they know the price. Conversely, value buyers don't care about the price until they've determined whether your offering is going to meet their needs.

Another way to ascertain buyers' predilections is to engage them in a discussion of other things they own. If the discussion revolves around the great deal they received, you're dealing with price buyers. If, however, they explain the various options they had and how they weighed those options in making their decision, they are value buyers.

A third approach is to observe your prospect's behavior during the sales call. Here's what I experienced on one of my sales calls. As you read this example, look for clues that help you discern whether the prospect is a price buyer or value buyer.

A prospective client invited me to meet with him and his partner to discuss the challenges they faced. We met in their office. The partner asked if it would be all right if we met near the copier so that he could "get a report assembled and out to a client."

One of *their* prospects surveyed the market and found that these guys were rated number one in quality, but was considering using a "cheaper" vendor. *My* prospect was giving serious consideration to dropping their price to get the business.

During the meeting, these two business owners told me that they were the rainmakers in their organization – they generated virtually all of the sales their company made.

The conversation drifted to one of their vendors, a vendor I had recommended to my clients. Their comment was, "It's a great service, but if it weren't for the savings on worker's compensation and health insurance, it would be expensive."

Are these guys price buyers or value buyers? What influenced your decision? Here's the analysis I went through.

These guys are the rainmakers in their organization, but they choose to perform a clerical task. Would you spend time doing a $12.00 an hour task when you could be generating ten times that or more in additional revenues? You would if you were a price buyer. As we discussed earlier, price buyers place greater value on saving money than generating revenues. This behavior indicates that they are price buyers.

They were willing to drop their price to get business even though *their prospect's survey* rated them number one in quality. I could have given them the benefit of the doubt and assumed that they simply didn't know how to quantify value, but my experience has been that value sellers, even those who aren't adept at quantifying value, walk away from prospects who are unwilling to pay for value that's readily apparent. The fact that these business owners were willing to lower their price indicates that they are price buyers.

Their comment, "It's a great service, but if it weren't for the savings on worker's compensation and health insurance, it would be expensive," is another indication that they are price buyers. The fact that they had outsourced their human resources function would, typically, be a sign that they are value buyers. Why? Because they had contracted for skills they didn't possess. They were, however, focusing only on the cost savings aspects of the service, not its ability to help them generate more revenues. That's why I say that this is another indication that they are price buyers.

By observing these two business owners, I could quickly discern that we were not going to be a good fit for one another. They are price buyers/sellers. I'm a value buyer/seller. The only thing our association could have achieved was frustration for all parties. As I shared my thoughts with them, they agreed that we weren't a good fit. We parted company on a friendly note – each respecting the other's right to the choices we made.

Now that you know how to evaluate your existing customers and future prospects, let's evaluate your sales force.

Evaluating and Recruiting Salespeople

The same tools you used to assess your natural style can be used in determining whether a salesperson is or will be a good fit for your organization. Why is that important? A poor fit:

- Increases frustration for you and your salespeople.
- Causes you to invest heavily in sales training that doesn't produce results.
- Increases the turnover rate in your sales force.

Let's take a closer look at each of these costly conditions.

Frustration

You and your salespeople will experience frustration any time there is a mismatch between the salesperson's natural style and your business strategy. Let's see what that frustration looks like for a value seller in a low-price environment.

Salespeople are typically compensated on either revenue dollars or profit dollars. A value seller likes to maximize revenue, or profit dollars, on each sale by getting higher prices for the value provided. If you're using a low-price strategy, your value sellers are going to feel that their income potential is limited. They are also going to resent it when you cave to a customer's request for a price reduction because each concession costs them money. You *will* make concessions regularly. It's your nature!

Conversely, a price seller in a value environment will feel pressure to sell up – to get better prices. That goes against this individual's nature and creates performance expectations he or she isn't likely to meet. A salesperson in this situation will live everyday in fear of losing his or her job. That doesn't do either of you any good.

You, too, will feel frustrated. If you're employing a low-price strategy, you'll feel that your value sellers are costing you business. Why? Because they aren't willing to come down on price to get the deal.

Your frustration is every bit as real when you're using a value strategy and your price sellers cave on price to get the business. You feel that you're leaving money on the table – not getting a good return on your marketing dollars, production effort, or the money you are paying the salesperson.

"Yes, yes," some of you are thinking, "I'll set the price and make my salespeople live with it." Nice theory, but not very practical. Value sellers won't find the limits on their income any less frustrating because the price is fixed. Nor will price sellers find it any less difficult to meet your sales expectations when they don't have the ability to make price concessions.

If the frustration weren't bad enough, you can spend a fortune on sales training and never get the desired result.

Wasted Training Dollars

As mentioned earlier, I do believe that people can overcome their natural tendencies. It is hard work, and it can take years to accomplish. Do you and your company have that kind of time? Are you willing to make that investment? Are your salespeople willing to invest their time and effort? The answer to these questions is "Probably not."

Unfortunately, many business owners don't have the insights you've just gained, so these questions don't get asked. Consequently, underperforming salespeople are dealt with in the following ways:

- They get more training.
- They're mentored (one-on-one assistance).
- They're moved to inside sales (assuming they're willing to take a pay cut).
- Their employment is terminated.

The last two options aren't as costly as the first two. Unfortunately, business owners typically don't consider these options until they've already spent a great deal of money on the first two.

Before I get into hot water with sales trainers, I'm not suggesting that sales training is bad. There are some excellent programs available. The money is wasted when you're trying to get salespeople to go against their nature – teaching price sellers to become value sellers or vice versa.

At some point, the frustration and wasted training dollars will take their toll, and you'll experience higher than usual turnover in your sales force.

Turnover

Good price sellers and good value sellers quickly realize when they're in the wrong environment and opt themselves out. Price sellers in a value environment realize that they're not likely to meet your expectations and seek a job with a company better aligned to their style. Similarly, a good value seller realizes the restrictions that a low-price environment places on his or her income and leaves quickly.

What about those who don't opt out on their own? Their lack of results is going to require you, at some point, to let them go. Regardless of whether the choice to leave is yours or theirs, your turnover rate goes up when you have a mismatch between your company's strategy and the salesperson's natural selling style. What are the costs associated with this turnover?

Every time that you have to replace a salesperson you lose:

- Consistency and credibility with your customers.
- Significant portions of the pipeline that salesperson generated.
- Sales momentum as your new salesperson gets acclimated.
- The training dollars spent on the exiting salesperson.
- Time and sales dollars as you or one of your successful salespeople mentor the new person.

These are hefty prices to pay. So far we've looked only at the dark side of a mismatch. It's time to take a look at the advantages you gain from hiring the right style for your strategy.

Matching Styles

Low-price sellers are great if you have a low-price strategy. Why? Because they speak your customers' language. They won't waste time telling customers and prospects about the bells and whistles of your offerings; they'll get to the heart of the matter – price.

That doesn't mean that price sellers can't speak intelligently about other aspects of your offerings; they can. They will, however, minimize the importance of these benefits to keep the focus on price. Why?

Good salespeople know that buying decisions are made emotionally – that logic enters the picture only when buyers justify their decisions to others. That's why the price seller *must* minimize the importance of other aspects of your offerings to a price buyer – to provide the logic for the low-price purchase.

Value sellers working for a value-oriented company do just the opposite. They tout the other aspects of the offerings and minimize price. The value seller speaks the language of the value customers; it's the language of convenience, quality, dependability, integrity, friendliness, and guarantees.

Of course, the sale can't be completed without a discussion of price, but value sellers will minimize its importance while elevating the importance of other aspects of your offering. Like good price sellers, they realize that their prospects are looking for a way to justify their buying decisions. This time the buyer is trying to justify paying a higher price.

There is one more group that we need to address – professional management. Earlier, in the "Nature and Strategy" section of this chapter, I suggested that if you're a price buyer/seller it would be advantageous to hire value-oriented professional management. How do you determine whether a professional manager has a value orientation?

Professional Management

Is the process any different for professional managers than for salespeople? It's a little different. Professional managers may not have sales experience, so observing them in a sales call might not be helpful. Questions about their buying habits may raise an eyebrow or two, so you may want to stay away from that. So what can you do?

First, make sure that the candidates had the ability to influence pricing in their previous employments. Then ask the following questions:

- Do you have experience in business development? If not, ask the candidates to name two companies they admire. Why those two companies?
- If the candidates have sales experience, what was the key to their success?
- How did their company's pricing compare to their competitors' pricing?
- What was their company's policy regarding price increases? How effective were they in implementing that policy?
- Were the candidates able to increase productivity?
- If they increased productivity, what was their motivation? Was it to reduce the price to the customer, increase capacity, or cut costs?
- Ask them how they determined which operating activities to keep in house and which to outsource? What was their rationale?

Here's what you can glean from the answers you get.

Admired Companies

From these questions, you can discern the candidates' attitudes toward pricing. If their favorite companies are WalMart and Southwest Airlines, they have a price orientation. If they are Nordstrom's and Ritz-Carlton, they are value buyers. If the companies they mention fall between these two extremes, their reasons for admiring these companies will indicate whether they are price or value buyers.

Sales Experience

Those with sales experience will tell you all you need to know when they tell you how their prices stacked up against their competitors' pricing. If the prices were at or below industry pricing, they're likely to be price buyers. If their prices were above the industry average, odds are good that they're value buyers.

Pricing Policy

Companies that follow an established policy of increasing prices tend to be value sellers. Those that don't, tend to be price buyers.

Productivity

The productivity questions go to motivation. Why did they increase productivity? Was it to offer lower prices than their competitors? If so, they are price buyers. Was their purpose to increase capacity so they could generate more sales at existing prices? Value buyer. If their primary goal was simply to cut costs, they are definitely price buyers.

Too often I hear business owners lament the fact that their customers are 900-pound gorillas that won't let them increase prices. These owners always have the choice of walking away, so don't let your candidates get by with this excuse. It may be the reason they're looking for a job.

Outsourcing

Asking candidates which services they kept in house and which they outsourced is another reliable indicator of their buying style. Again, we're looking for motivation. Why did they decide to keep something in-house? Here's a sample question.

Did they outsource payroll processing? This is one service for which outsourcing makes perfect sense. The laws change frequently enough to make it challenging to keep up with them, plus there are severe penalties involved if you make a mistake. Payroll services provide a guarantee – if they make a mistake, they pay the fines. If your candidates outsource payroll, not only did they avoid the hassle of keeping up with the law, they shifted risk to someone else. Good move! Outsourcing payroll services could indicate that they are value buyers. Can we assume that the opposite is true as well? Does a decision not to outsource payroll processing make them price buyers?

Not necessarily. There are valid reasons not to outsource payroll. One of my clients does its own payroll processing. Why? The company is in the construction industry; its ability to monitor labor productivity on each project is essential to its success. Payroll services typically aren't as effective as in-house operations in providing real-time information.

Keeping payroll in-house makes sense for this client because it allows its managers to monitor productivity and customer expectations more effectively. This company is a value buyer. If, however, my client was processing payroll because management felt the service was too expensive, it would be an indication that it was a price buyer.

As you can see, it's fairly easy to discern whether a professional manager is a price buyer or value buyer. Remember, it's not enough to hire a value buyer to run your business or at least that portion that deals with pricing and sales. You must stay out of his or her way. If you don't, the only thing you'll accomplish is increasing your overhead.

So far, you've learned how to:

- Assess your natural style.
- Assess the natural styles of your customers and prospects.
- Assess your salespeople's and future candidates' natural styles.
- Use your natural style to define an effective pricing strategy.
- Build a value-based organization when your natural orientation is price.

Before we move onto Chapter 3, let's review why a low-price strategy is so costly.

The High Cost of Low Prices

Low-price strategies have several costly disadvantages for the business owner:

- Price buyers are not loyal; replacing lost customers is expensive.
- Costs, once cut, tend to creep up again, leaving the company in a position of covering "normal" industry costs with low prices.
- At some point, the cost of achieving further cuts outweighs the benefits – two examples are WalMart's legal problems and Southwest Airlines' fines.
- You have a limited market - only 14 percent of the buying public considers price the number one criteria in their buying decisions; 86 percent prefer value over price.

There are nonmonetary costs as well. First, controlling costs isn't much fun. Few business owners awaken thinking "I get to cut costs today!" It's not what drives them. What does drive them?

They love to create new offerings, apply new technologies, locate new markets, and WOW their customers. There passion doesn't lie with cost control. It's this lack of passion that allows cost cuts, once made, to creep up again. That's what makes a low-price strategy so expensive for the majority of business owners.

Let's not forget the cost to buyers. We, as consumers, ultimately pay the price for low-price strategies. Subprime losses, American Airlines flight cancellation costs, WalMart's settlements, and Southwest Airlines' fines will all be borne by the consumer. How?

The subprime costs will be covered by higher interest rates, additional loan fees, and higher closing costs. The American and Southwest Airline costs will appear as higher ticket prices, protracted travel times (costing us revenues and productivity), and higher taxes to cover the cost of government oversight.

Enough of the gloom and doom! Let's learn how to quantify value. On to Chapter 3!

Executive Summary

1. A person's buying habits are a mirror image of his or her sales style. Price buyers are price sellers; value buyers sell value.
2. Know thyself. Are you a price buyer or a value buyer? Do those close to you agree with your assessment? Here are three ways to tell:
   - Self-evaluation.
   - Buyer-evaluation questions to ask those closest to you.
   - Seller-evaluation questions to ask those who have observed you in sales situations.
3. Nature and strategy: your business strategy should reflect your natural style. If your style and strategy are low price, populate your organization with people who are passionate about cost control. If you want a value-based organization, hire value-minded professionals.
4. Evaluate your customers/prospects. Are they price buyers or value buyers?
   - Is price one of the first questions they ask?

- When they describe other purchases they've made, do they talk about the great deal they got or do they discuss the analysis they went through in the decision-making process?
- Do they consistently spend more time on tasks that "save" money rather than those that "generate" income?

5. Use the questions in #4 to identify the right salespeople for your organization.

6. Discern a professional managers' buying style. Ask the following questions:
   - Do they have experience in business development? If not, ask them to name two companies whose business strategy they admire. Why those two companies?
   - If they have business development experience, what was the key to their success? How did their pricing compare to your competitors' pricing?
   - What was their policy regarding price increase? Why did it work or not?
   - Have they been able to increase productivity?
   - If they increased productivity, what was their motivation: to reduce the price to the customer, increase capacity, or simply cut costs?
   - Ask them how they determine which operating activities to keep in house and which to outsource? What's their rationale?

7. There are significant costs, monetary and nonmonetary, to you, your customers, and the buying public when you choose a low-price strategy.

3

Elementary School Math: Quantifying Value

If you've ever helped your child, grandchild, nephew, or niece with their homework, you've observed them struggling with concepts that are second nature to you. The goal of this chapter is to make converting the intrinsic value of your offerings—your goods and services—into dollars and cents as natural as elementary school math is for you today.

As with any skill, daily practice is needed for the skill to become "natural." I'll make a deal with you. I'll provide the tools, you dedicate practice time. Sound fair?

The first tool we need is an understanding of what customers really value.

Value

Value is a nebulous concept. It means different things to different people. What do buyers value?

- Speed
- Friendliness
- Integrity
- Dependability
- Convenience

- Image
- Service
- Innovation
- Knowledgeable salespeople

As you read each of the items on this list, you probably recalled purchases that you have made based on that value proposition. Your trip to Burger King was predicated on only having 20 minutes before your next meeting. You chose your bank because they greet you by name when you walk in the door. You bought your pickup truck from the salesperson who explained towing capacity, hauling capacity, differentials, gear ratios, cooling systems, and suspension.

In each of these purchases, a different value dictated your choice. Speed dictated your stop at Burger King; friendliness, your choice of a bank; a knowledgeable salesperson, your truck purchase. The fact that every customer values all of the items on the list leaves us, as business owners, feeling like we're in a desert of ever-shifting sands. The landscape is always changing, yet we're expected to be consistent in our pricing. It isn't fair! Or is it?

Are things as they appear? Are customer preferences constantly changing? When they do change, do customers really expect the price to remain unchanged? The answers may surprise you.

Are Things as They Appear?

The complexity of "customer preferences" is a fabrication of our minds, not of our customers' minds. Do you think McDonald's customers expect anything but consistency and speed? Does a Nordstrom customer want a wool sweater or the personal service Nordstrom provides? Does the Chivas Regal drinker want scotch whiskey or a taste experience?

The reality is that only one or two aspects of your offering have real value to your customers. The rest are merely nice to have. If you doubt that, the next time a customer asks for something special, attach a price to it. If they pay, they truly value what they've requested. If they refuse to pay, the request was merely an attempt to see how good a deal they could get. Buyers will not be denied what they truly desire; they will find the money if it's important enough to them.

Are Customer Preferences Constantly Changing?

They do change, but not constantly. Most of the change in customer preferences is our creation. It's born of attempts to differentiate our offerings from those of our competitors. Our competitors match our quality, so we speed up our delivery. They match our delivery times, so we add a new dimension to our service. They match our service, so we build more quality into our product. Round and round we go on the "not-so-merry" merry-go-round.

The perception is that our customers' preferences are changing when, in reality, we're offering enhancements to retain their business. We do it without asking for more money. Customers graciously accept these offers. Why not? It doesn't cost them anything.

It's not our customers' preferences that are changing constantly. It's our desire to maintain a competitive advantage that drives us to continuously offer new benefits. When we look back on how our offerings have changed over time, we mistakenly ascribe the changes to shifting customer preferences.

The key to avoiding this dilemma is to attach a price tag to any new benefit you offer. If your customers are willing to pay extra to get that benefit, they value it. If not, keep looking until you find something they do value. That brings us to our third question: do customers expect the price to change?

When Customer Preferences Change, Do Customers Expect the Price to Change?

The quick answer is "Yes." How can I be so sure? Think back to a time when you were the customer making a special request. I'm willing to bet that your request included the phrase, "I'm willing to pay extra."

Customers understand that there are costs and risks associated with providing something outside your "normal" offering. They understand it, they respect it and, if it's important enough to them, they'll pay for it. If it's not important enough for them to part with their money, it shouldn't be important to you.

As you can see, the constantly shifting sands of "customer preferences" are of our own making. Now that we have an approach for determining what customers value, let's figure out how much they're willing to pay for what they value.

What Customers Value

For your convenience, I've listed the nine value propositions we discussed earlier:

- Speed
- Friendliness

- Integrity
- Dependability

- Convenience
- Image
- Service
- Innovation
- Knowledgeable salespeople

This is not an all-inclusive list. There may be aspects of your offerings that aren't included. That won't be a problem. The approach used in identifying what customers value and how much value they place on that attribute can easily be adapted to your offerings.

My experience has been that most offerings include anywhere from two to four of the aforementioned value attributes. That makes calculating value a daunting task. When you consider the number of products/services you provide, calculating value becomes a seemingly impossible task. Let's see if we can simplify the process for you.

We'll begin by looking at each value attribute to see if they have anything in common. Specifically, we're going to look at what benefit each attribute affords. Table 3-1 shows the results of this analysis.

By viewing the nine value propositions through the lens of the benefits each provides, we discover that there are only three benefits and, consequently, only three calculations needed to monetize the value of your offerings. Those benefits are image, innovation, and time savings.

The process becomes even simpler when we realize that there is typically one attribute that converts prospects to customers. In the case of a convenience store, it's time savings. You might like the fact that the store is clean, has esthetically appealing signage, and a friendly staff, but they're bonuses. The real reason you're willing to pay premium prices at a convenience store is that it saves you time.

What about your doctor? What is it about your doctor that you value? Most of us would like to think we chose our doctor on the basis of his or her medical knowledge. The reality is that those of us outside the medical community don't have a clue how to evaluate a doctor's ability. We *choose* a doctor based on:

- convenience (time savings).
- a friend's recommendation (dependability = time savings).
- image (my doctor is the top thoracic surgeon in the country).

Table 3-1. Value Attribute/Benefit Relationship

Value Attribute	Benefit Enjoyed
Speed	Time savings – It's the reason we go to fast-food restaurants, Jiffy Lube, or any vendor in any industry that offers quick service.
Friendliness	Image – Isn't friendliness really about image? Don't you frequent businesses that demonstrate genuine joy at having you in their shop because they make you feel good about yourself?
Integrity	Time savings – How much longer does it take you to make a buying decision when you're not sure you can trust the person with whom you're dealing? What's the likelihood of having to take the item back because the offering was misrepresented to you? How much time do you lose when have to take the item back or, in the case of service, spend time doing the project yourself? Dealing with someone with integrity saves you time.
Dependability	Time savings – How much time does it save you when an auto repair shop fixes your problem right the first time? How much time do you lose when you buy an inexpensive product and have to replace it every few months instead of every few years? How much time does your company lose when a supplier ships product that doesn't meet specifications?
Convenience	Time savings – How much time do you save by picking up milk at the gas station instead of making a separate stop at the grocery store?
Image	Image – It's why people shop Saks Fifth Avenue, own Mercedes-Benz cars, and 10,000+ square foot homes on five-acre tracts. These purchases tout the buyer's success and passion for "the finer things in life."
Innovation	Image/innovation – Some buyers are big kids who just enjoy playing with new toys. Others want to be viewed as leading edge people (image). Some buyers want both.
Knowledgeable salesperson	Time savings – Knowledgeable salespeople save you time. They help you identify what you really want and offer only what fits. The others waste your time trying to impress you with features that have no value to you.

We *stay* with a doctor because he or she:

- Takes time to explain things to us (knowledgeable, dependable = time savings).
- Is friendly and caring (image).
- Respects our time (time savings).

Clearly, these three benefits are readily adaptable to any business or profession. The key is identifying the one attribute that keeps your customers coming back. We'll discuss this more in Chapters 4 and 5. For now, let's learn how to calculate value.

Calculating Value

We've narrowed the number of calculations needed to three – image, innovation, and time savings. There may be more than one approach to each of these calculations, but there is only one calculation that you'll need to make to monetize the value of your offering. Let's begin with image.

Image

The esoteric nature of image doesn't lend itself to precise mathematical calculation. Fortunately we don't need a precise formula. We can glean how much people are willing to pay for image by observing the premiums they pay for other image-enhancing purchases.

It would be nice if all customers valued image equally, but we know that's not the case. So let's look at how companies, whose primary value attribute is image, have positioned their pricing versus the general market and within their own offerings. These comparisons will allow us to extrapolate a range of pricing premiums available to you. Armed with this data, we'll craft an approach that you can use to determine the premiums you should be getting for your offerings.

We'll begin by examining image premiums on things virtually everyone buys – clothing, automobiles, and electronics.

Clothing

With clothing, image lies primarily in the designer's name. Store ambiance and personal service add even more value to image. Let's take a

Table 3-2. Impact of Image on Clothing Prices

Store	Image Offered	Price Comparisons
WalMart	No designer brands	Lowest price
Target	Emerging designers	2× the WalMart price
Macy's	Designer brands, some service	4× the WalMart price
Nordstrom's Saks Fifth Avenue	Designer brands, luxurious ambiance, exceptional personal service	10× the WalMart price

look at several well-known retailers in Table 3-2 to see how much image is a part of their offerings and what their buyers pay for the image they get.

The above comparisons were based on a random sampling of items – slacks, dresses, shirts, sweaters, and so on. As you can see, the premiums people pay for image are huge – as much as ten times the lowest price available. We'll discuss how to use this information to create your pricing policy once we've reviewed all three purchases. Let's see what the premiums are for automobiles.

Automobiles

We're going to make two comparisons. In Table 3-3, we compare Mercedes', Lexus', and Cadillac's smallest luxury sedans with three other manufacturers' smallest, least expensive sedans. In Table 3-4, we compare the various size luxury cars that Mercedes, Lexus, and Cadillac offer and the premiums people are willing to pay for the larger models.

Before we start, I want to acknowledge that each of us has a different comfort level with math. Also, there are some ways of looking at numbers that are easier for us to understand than others. To make the following tables easier to read and understand, let me review a couple of quick math concepts. Please forgive me if you are experienced with these concepts, but I want to make sure that every reader finds the information in the following tables useful.

There are two ways that people make price comparisons. They either express the price relation as a percentage (Product A is 20 percent more than that Product B) or as multiple (Product B is 1.2 times as much Product A). Both statements say the same thing.

Typically, people don't have a problem making this translation from 20 percent more to 1.2 times or vice versa when the percentages are lower than 100 percent. Confusion creeps in when the percentages are higher than 100 percent, which is not unusual with premium pricing – especially when it relates to image.

We can illustrate the source of the confusion with this simple example. We're going to assume that Product A's price is $10 and Product B's price is $100. Let's calculate the multiple first since it's a little easier. Product B is ten times the cost Product A. All we did was divide B's price of $100 by A's price of $10:

$$\$100/\$10 = 10$$

Let's contrast that with the percentage approach. The percentage approach looks at how much *more* you're paying for Product B than Product A. To convert the price differential into a percentage, we use a two-step process. First we calculate the differential; then we divide the differential by the price of the lower-priced product. Staying with our examples, here are the calculations:

$$\$100 - \$10 = \$90 \text{ price differential}$$
$$\$90/\$10 = 9 \text{ or } 900\% \ (9 \times 100\%)$$

The confusion comes when people try to translate this percentage into a price multiple. They think "The price is 900 percent higher, so Product B is nine times Product A." In actuality, it's ten times higher, as we saw in our calculation of the multiple. People using the percentage approach forget that they're calculating how much *more* they're paying, instead of what they're paying in total. Just remember that when you use the percentage method and convert that number to a multiple, you need to add 1 to that total to get the true multiple you're paying. Here's what the formulae would look like if the conversion were done correctly.

$$\$100 - \$10 = \$90 \text{ price differential}$$
$$\$90/\$10 = 9 \text{ or } 900\% (9 \times 100\% \text{ higher price})$$
$$900\% \text{ incremental price} + 100\% \text{ base price} = 1{,}000\%$$
$$1{,}000\%/100\% = 10 \text{ (price multiple)}$$

In the following tables I'll show both the percentage increase in price and the price multiple so that you don't have wrestle with these conversions.

Table 3-3 compares the prices of the smallest Mercedes, Lexus, and Cadillac luxury sedans to three small, economy sedans. To keep the math simple in both Tables 3-3 and 3-4, I've rounded the manufacturers' suggested retail price up or down to the nearest $500.

Again, we see huge premiums (100 percent to 196 percent) for luxury cars over economy cars. This isn't the whole story though. Mercedes, Lexus, and Cadillac also have mid- and full-sized models. Let's see what kind of premium they carry.

Obviously, when it comes to luxury cars, size does matter. Cadillac is the only luxury brand in this example that isn't charging at least twice the price of its smaller model. To get a sense for the full potential of image, let's compare Mercedes S-Class to our three economy cars (Table 3-5).

Table 3-3. Price Premiums – Small Luxury Cars Versus Economy Cars

	Mercedes C-Class $34,000	Lexus IS09 $31,000	Cadillac CTS $37,000
Ford Focus *$15,000*	127% higher 2.27×	107% higher 2.07×	147% higher 2.47×
GM Aveo *$12,500*	172% higher 2.72×	148% higher 2.48×	196% higher 2.96×
Toyota Corolla *$15,500*	119% higher 2.19×	100% higher 2.00×	139% higher 2.39%

Table 3-4. Impact of Luxury Auto Size on Image and Prices

Size	Mercedes	Lexus	Cadillac
Small	C-Class $34,000	IS09 $31,000	CTS $37,000
Mid-size	E-Class $54,000	GS09 $45,000	STS $48,500
Mid-size vs. small	59% higher	45% higher	31% higher
	1.59×	1.45×	1.31×
Full size	S-Class $90,000	LS09 $63,500	DTS $55,500
Full size vs. small	165% higher	105% higher	50% higher
	2.65×	2.05×	1.50×

Table 3-5. Full Luxury Sedan Versus Economy Sedan

Ford Focus $15,000	GM Aveo $12,500	Toyota Corolla $15,500
Mercedes S-Class $90,000	Mercedes S-Class $90,000	Mercedes S-Class $90,000
500% higher	620% higher	480%
6×	7.2×	5.8×

The multiples aren't quite as high as those enjoyed by Nordstrom and Saks, but given the price differential (a few hundred dollars vs. $90,000) they're huge. On to electronics!

Electronics

What image premiums await us in the electronics world? I've chosen home theater systems for this example. One of the reasons behind this choice is that most of us, unless we're making side-by-side comparisons, couldn't tell the difference in quality if our lives depended on it. If we're incapable of enjoying the additional quality, what reason is there for buying the top-of-the-line other than image? Here's how three popular brands – Bose, Sony, and Samsung - stack up.

Table 3-6. Price Premiums - Home Theater Systems

Home Theater Systems	Bose	Sony's Bravia 5.1 channel system	Samsung 5.1 channel system
Entry level	$1,000	$200	$400
Top of the line	$3,800	$700	$900
Top line vs. entry level	280% higher	250% higher	125% higher
	3.8×	3.5×	2.25×
Bose's entry premium		400%	150%
		5×	2.5×
Bose's top line premium		442%	322%
		5.42×	4.22×

The prices in Table 3-6 are the result of comparing the prices of several well-known electronics retailers and have been rounded to nearest $100 to make the calculations simpler.

Bose is king of the hill, with multiples running 4 to 5.5 times (300 percent to 450 percent higher) than the popular Sony and Samsung brands. The one exception is Samsung's entry-level product. The multiples on these home theater systems aren't as high as those on clothing and automobiles, but they're still impressive. What do these premiums mean for your bottom line?

Profit implications

Bose needs one-fifth the customers that Sony does to generate the same revenue dollars. Mercedes needs to sell only one S-Class sedan for every seven Aveos. Nordstrom and Saks need one-tenth the customers that WalMart does.

Imagine how much infrastructure cost in the form of physical plant, office space, employee wages, leadership compensation, inventory, and marketing are required to serve two, seven, or ten times the number of customers your competitor does. That's an unheralded benefit of premium pricing. You don't have to attract and retain huge numbers of customers to generate the same revenue and a ton more profit.

Now that I have that off my chest, let's get back to calculating the value of image.

Return to Image Pricing

I've created Table 3-7 to show the kind of impact household income and size of purchase *typically* have on price multiples. The information in Table 3-7 is extrapolated from the data in our clothing, automobile, and home theater system examples above and personal experience in helping clients with price their offerings. (*Note:* Table 3-7 is *not* to be used to establish pricing. It is merely intended to give you a sense of how household income and item cost affect image premiums. We'll get to the actual calculations in a moment).

What Table 3-7 illustrates is that the premiums low- and middle-income households are willing to pay for image are much lower than for high-income households. Indeed, we can reasonably expect high-income households to pay roughly five times the premium for image that the $25,000 to $50,000 income folks do. That's why companies selling to higher income families build image enhancement into their offerings.

You've also noticed that the premiums decline for all income levels as the price tag goes up. I doubt that you're surprised by that fact. The higher the price tag, the more months or years of income the purchase absorbs. Thus, the premium we're willing to pay drops.

Image Formulae

Armed with these insights into the size and pattern of premium pricing, we're ready to develop an image pricing model for *your* business. Here's what you need to do:

1. Determine how important image is to your customers? Are they Target, Macy's or Nordstrom buyers? Do they buy Aveos or Mercedes S-Class sedans? Is their home theater system Bose or Sony?

    Don't limit your investigation to one or two items that they buy. Use various price points and types of products/services to get a sense of their attitude toward image. Why? Each of us has our petty economies, purchases that we don't want to make but can't avoid, so we spend as little as possible.

Table 3-7. Impact of Household Income and Item Cost on Image Premium

Price Range– No Image Value	Image Importance	Annual Household Income	Price Multiple	Price
$1 – $999	Modest	$25,000 – $50,000	2x	$2 – $1,998
	Moderate	$50,001 – $100,000	4x	$4 – $3,996
	Primary	$100,000+	10x	$10 – $9,990
$1,000 to $4,999	Modest	$25,000 – $50,000	1.75x	$1,750 – $8,748
	Moderate	$50,001 – $100,000	3.5x	$3,500 – $17,497
	Primary	$100,000+	9x	$9,000 – $44,991
$5,000 to $9,999	Modest	$25,000 – $50,000	1.5x	$7,500 – $14,999
	Moderate	$50,001 – $100,000	2.75x	$13,750 – $27,497
	Primary	$100,000+	8x	$40,000 – $79,992
$10,000+	Modest	$25,000 – $50,000	1.25x	$12,500 on up
	Moderate	$50,001 – $100,000	2x	$20,000 on up
	Primary	$100,000+	7x	$70,000 on up

    Conversely, there are things for which we'll pay handsomely because it's what we really want – the brand new $30,000 pickup truck in front a mobile home. If we don't examine an adequate number of buying decisions that our customers make, we open ourselves to erroneous conclusions about the value image has to them.

2. Research companies in noncompeting industries that target the same customer you do and have similar price points. If I were Nordstrom, I wouldn't compare my price multiples to Mercedes, as the prices are too disparate – a few hundred dollars to a $1,000 vs. $30,000 to $90,000 for an automobile. If I made that comparison, I'd leave money on the table. Instead, I'd compare my prices to Godiva and Ghirardelli chocolates or A.H. Hirsch bourbon whiskey. The price points are much closer and they have that top-of-the-line image presence.

3. Using the information from these noncompeting companies, determine the price multiples they use at various price points (assuming they offer multiple levels of image enhancement). The results of your analysis can easily be put into a table format like that of Table 3-7.

4. Decide which of those price points you're going to target and use the highest price multiple you find. This is not the time to be modest. If your offering is superior, you should be compensated more than anyone else.

5. Multiply the premium multiple in Step 4 by the price of the bare bones, no-frills-attached offering in your industry. In essence, you're going to be looking at the WalMart or Aveo in your industry. You're going to apply your multiple to their prices to establish your price.

Now that you now have a methodology for calculating the image value of your offerings, let's turn our attention to innovation.

Innovation

When we look at the market for innovation we see three categories of buyers:

- *Early adopters* – those who love being on the leading edge and regaling others with stories of the obstacles they overcame as early adopters.
- *Dependability buyers* – those who buy once the product or service has proven to work consistently.
- *Late adopters* – those who are "forced" into accepting new products/ services because their previous choice is no longer available.

What price are these buyers willing to pay? Let's go back to the example I used in Chapter 1, VCR and DVD players. Both have run the cycle from new technology to market saturation. Both followed the same pricing path. How much did each buyer pay?

- Early adopters $1,000
- Dependability buyers $400
- Late adopters $100

The early adopters paid 2.5 times what the dependability buyers did and a whopping ten times what the late adopters did. Again, these are only two products. We can't translate that into a pricing policy you can use. We can, however, modify the image approach and perform similar calculations to get you higher compensation for your innovations.

Innovation Formulae
Here are the steps involved in calculating the value of innovation.

1. Determine how important innovation is to the market you're targeting or want to target. Are they early adopters, dependability buyers, or late adopters?
2. Research innovation companies in noncompeting industries that target the same customer group you do and have similar price points. What do you want to learn?

    - Where they set their price point when launching a new offering.
    - How long it takes for dependability buyers to enter the market, and what price they're willing to pay.

- How long it takes for late adopters to make their first purchase, and what price they typically pay.

3. Next, calculate the price premiums that early adopters and dependability buyers pay over what the late adopters pay in these noncompeting businesses.

4. Take the highest early adopter and dependability buyer multiples that you found in the noncompeting businesses you researched, assuming that they are higher than yours, and apply them to the late adopter price for your offerings to set prices for the early adopters and dependability buyers. You'll be surprised to find that the additional multiples have little, if any, effect on the number of early adopters you attract.

    If you do experience some small decline, the premiums that you make on the remaining early adopters will more than offset the revenue lost from those who shifted to the dependability buyer category. That's right! You don't lose these customers; they simply moved down one category on the scale.

    This step presumes that you are an innovator – that you aren't simply copying someone else's innovation. The true innovator is the only one who has the opportunity to establish price on the innovation. Those who follow cannot get prices higher than those set by the innovator.

5. Monitor the market's perception of the dependability of your offering. When your offering is field proven, lower your price to reflect the dependability buyer premium. That will allow you to be the first to attract the general market. The more quickly you can attract the general market, the more difficult you make it for your competitors. Once the general market associates your name with innovation and dependability, it's tough for a competitor to lure them away.

6. Keep a strong pipeline of innovation going. The most successful innovators are those that obsolete their own offerings. Hewlett Packard's printers and Intel's chips (Intel Inside) are classic examples. Each company enjoyed its greatest success when it launched new products just as its competitors were about to catch up to the last innovation. What do you gain by employing these practices?

- Your competitors never get the premium pricing the early adopters pay.
- You gain a loyal following from early adopters.
- You gain the lion's share of the dependability buyers.
- You generate incredible profits and cash flow.

Now that we've discovered how to calculate the value of image and innovation, let's move on to time savings.

Time Savings

I've divided this section into two subsections, business to retail and business to business, because what we do with time savings depends heavily on whether it's personal time or company time. We'll begin with business to retail.

Business to Retail

On the surface, saving time seems like a pretty easy calculation. All we need to know is:

- How much time are we going to save?
- What's the value of our time?

Just how valuable is your time? That depends on how you're going to use it. There are basically two ways that people use time – to make money or for recreation. Which is more valuable? I'm sure most of you said "Recreation!" You're absolutely right. Let's see what the relative values are.

Earn More Money   If you use the time you save to make more money, how much do you expect to make? Many people feel that if they can't make at least as much as they do in their job, they're just going to kick back and relax or spend time on their favorite hobby. They're not going to work.

The exception is when there are money-making opportunities associated with their hobby. An avid bass fisherman might sign up for fishing tournaments or a craft artist might purchase a booth at craft festivals. The fact that they might not earn as much as they do at work doesn't bother them, because it's their hobby. The money they make is simply a way to finance the hobby without reducing their lifestyle.

Earn More Money Formula   How do we calculate the value of time for people whose goal is to earn more money? It's simple; it's the hourly rate of pay they get at work. Knowing your customer's annual income allows you to calculate the customer's hourly rate and revenue-generating potential. Why not add a premium to the hourly rate?

   If customer's employees knew how to make more money in their regular jobs, they'd do it. Or, if they do know how, the additional compensation they'd get isn't worth the tradeoffs they'd have to make. Either way, there is no premium available in this calculation. That's not the case with recreation.

Recreation   There are two approaches that buyers use in calculating the recreational value of time. One involves comparing their hourly rate versus the time savings associated with the offering – trading time. The other compares the enjoyment of their favorite activity with the cost of the offering. Most buyers do both calculations, often without realizing it.

   The most striking example of a person comparing current compensation to price came during a softball game. I was playing in a recreational league where the wives regularly attended. One of the women was the mother of fourteen; she didn't work outside the home. Her husband was a commercial heating/air-conditioning technician which, at that time, meant that he was making about $70,000 per year, including overtime.

   I overheard this woman tell the other women "I don't buy cut up chickens. I'm not going to pay someone to do something I can do myself." She did simple math. She weighed her income potential against the cost of paying someone else to perform the task.

   Indeed, it's a calculation each of us makes when we're considering paying for additional service – for additional time savings. We simply take our current level of compensation and compare it to the cost of having someone else do it. Voilà! It's worth it or it's not.

   Let's alter the facts in the above example slightly. We have a mother of two who works outside the home making $20,000 a year ($10/hour). Will she pay for cut up chickens? Cut chicken is 40¢ a pound more than the whole chicken. At $10 an hour, she's making 17¢ a minute. If it takes her more than 2.5 minutes to cut up that chicken, it's not worth her time.

The mind is amazing. We make these calculations so quickly and effortlessly that we don't even realize what we've done. The key is to know when your customers are using this approach to make their buying decisions. Why? They undervalue your offering. As you surmised earlier, the greatest value lies in recreation. You need to focus their attention on the recreational use of their time. How much more can you make?

In the example above, if you asked either mother what it would be worth to have an extra ten minutes to read a bedtime story to her children, she'd say "priceless." That's the calculation you want your customers to make. Here's another example of a priceless activity.

I've done a lot of work in the construction industry. I can tell you that in November it's virtually impossible to find a tradesmen. Why? It's deer hunting season. The thrill of the hunt, the ability to swap lies with close friends, and a short season combine to make this activity significantly more valuable than their hourly compensation.

Priceless doesn't help us develop a pricing strategy, though. So let's look at what kinds of premiums people pay for these "priceless" experiences.

I'm not a hunter myself. I really don't know what a hunting trip costs, so I'm going to shift to a recreational activity with which I have some familiarity – golf.

Let's say that you're a recreational golfer; you only play a few times a year. What are those outings worth to you? A round of golf at your favorite course costs $75. You probably spend another $40 on lunch, drinks, and side bets. So you spend $115 total. Since a typical eighteen-hole round of golf typically takes four hours, your cost is $28.75 per hour. How does that stack up against your income? The answer lies in Table 3-8.

Remember, you have only a passing interest in golf. Let's see what avid golfers might pay. First, they are likely to play at more challenging, esthetically appealing courses. Their greens fees would probably be closer to $110. Lunch, drinks, and more serious betting with their friends might cost $80 dollars. Their total cost $190, or $47.50 an hour. What kind of premium is an avid golfer paying?

Table 3-8. Value of Golf Outing to Recreational Golfer Versus Hourly Compensation

Annual Income	Hourly Rate	$28.75 Cost vs. Hourly Rate	Price Multiple
$ 30,000	$15	92% more	1.92x
$ 50,000	$25	15% more	1.15x
$ 70,000	$35	18% less	.82x
$100,000	$50	42% less	.58x

Table 3-9. Value of Golf Outing to Avid Golfer Versus Hourly Compensation

Annual Income	Hourly Rate	$47.50 Cost vs. Hourly Rate	Price Multiple
$ 30,000	$15	217% more	3.17×
$ 50,000	$25	90% more	1.90×
$ 70,000	$35	36% more	1.36×
$100,000	$50	5% less	.95×

What conclusions can we reach from these examples? Recreational golfers are willing to spend the equivalent of their hourly income or more for an outing. How do we know that? The first three income levels in Table 3-8 show that the $28.75/hour cost is at or above the golfer's hourly compensation.

Avid golfers, however, are willing to pay from one to three times their hourly rate (Table 3-9). I'm sure some of you are thinking, "Somebody making $30,000 a year isn't going to spend $190 playing golf." Have you forgotten the new $30,000 pickup in front of the mobile home?

People find the money to enjoy what they want. When you make assumptions about what people will or won't pay, you'll inevitably underestimate the value of your offerings. Let's translate these concepts into a pricing approach.

Recreational Pricing Formulae The following step-by-step process enables you to determine a price premium for those customers who value recreation over making more money:

1. Remember that buyers typically pay their hourly rate of compensation if they're trading time (having someone else do the work versus doing the work themselves).
2. Recall that buyers will pay two to three times their hourly rate to enjoy their favorite activity.
3. Focus your buyers' attention on spending time on their favorite activity, instead of merely trading dollars.
4. As you visualize your ideal customers, focus on their household income and level of interest in what you're offering.
5. Choose the appropriate price premium – one times their hourly rate if they're trading time, two times if they have recreational interest in the alternative activity, and three times or more if they're passionate about their favorite activity.
6. Multiply the appropriate premium times their hourly rate.

This simple approach will help you establish your price. In Chapter 5, you'll learn how to offer options and expand the number of price points you have for attracting customers.

Now that we've developed a pricing approach for those who value time savings in the business to retail sector, let's turn to business to business. The approaches share some similar elements, yet have slightly different formulae. Let's see how they stack up.

Business to Business
Business owners typically care about three things:

1. Can you help me generate more revenue?
2. Can you increase the productivity of my work force?
3. Can you help me cut costs?

If you can help them accomplish any of the three, they're interested.

Cutting Costs

Let's begin with cutting costs. It has the least benefit for your customers. Why? Cut costs rarely remain cut. It's like your diet. You set a goal to lose 20 pounds, work diligently to get there, and then . . . ? You ease off the exercise program, "treat yourself" to all those wonderful foods you've been depriving yourself of for the last two months, and regain the weight. Been there, done that!

Cutting costs is the equivalent of a corporate diet. Once the goal has been achieved, we breathe a sigh of relief, focus our attention elsewhere and, gradually, see costs rise as we return to old habits. If you're looking for evidence, you need look no further than the endless cycle of hiring and downsizing we've seen in the world's largest corporations for the past three decades.

If your goal is to provide value to your customer, don't sell them on the idea of cutting costs. Shift their focus to increasing productivity.

Increasing Productivity

Some of you may be wondering "Aren't they the same thing?" The answer is "No." Cutting costs reduces expenditures. Increasing productivity adds to revenue potential. If your organization currently generates $1 million in revenues, and you improve productivity by 20 percent, it can now generate $1.2 million in revenues *without adding any costs*. Increasing productivity creates the illusion of having cut costs when you really haven't. Table 3-10 shows us how business owners/leaders reach the erroneous conclusion that productivity increases reduce cost.

First, let me share with you the assumptions used in creating Table 3-10. I assumed that Any Company (our sample company):

- Increased productivity by 20 percent.
- Was able to generate enough sales to utilize this additional capacity.
- Was able to maintain its profit margins in generating those sales.
- Generated the additional revenue *without* adding costs.

Here are the results:

Table 3-10. Pre- and Postproductivity Increase Results

Any Company	Current Income Statement	Income and Expenses as a % of Revenues	Statement After Productivity Improvement	% After Productivity Improvement
Revenues	$1,000,000	100%	$1,200,000	100%
Cost of Goods Sold	$ 600,000	60%	$ 600,000	50%
Gross Profit	$ 400,000	40%	$ 600,000	50%
Selling, General and Administrative Expenses	$ 250,000	25%	$ 250,000	21%
Operating Income	$ 150,000	15%	$ 350,000	29%

Notice that the dollar amounts of both, the "Cost of Goods Sold" and "Selling, General and Administrative Expense" lines, remained the same. The percentages are a different story. The Cost of Goods Sold, as a percentage of revenues, dropped from 60 percent to 50 percent; Selling, General and Administrative Expenses dropped from 25 percent to 21 percent. If you were to look just at the percentages, you'd reach the conclusion that costs went down. They did, as a percentage of revenues, but not in absolute dollars.

As companies grow and the dollars get larger, managers rely more heavily on percentages to tell them when they're doing well and when they need to take corrective action. It's this propensity to use percentages that leaves many business owners/leaders equating cost cutting and productivity improvement.

Now that we understand why productivity enhancement is superior to cost cutting and why managers often confuse the two, let's see what how much value you can create for your customers.

Productivity is a function of labor. It's measured by comparing the revenues created to labor dollars expended. In the financial statements in Table 3-10, we see that there are two lines that include labor costs –

"Cost of Goods Sold" and "Selling, General and Administrative Expenses." If the value you provide is time savings, these are the two areas you're going to impact. Let's take a look at some of the ways in which you can help your customers save time.

In the Cost of Goods Sold area, you can help your customers:

1. Speed production by consistently meeting customers' specifications.
2. Minimize rework by building a high level of dependability into your offering.
3. Eliminate steps in the production process.
4. Maintain consistent production rates by meeting delivery deadlines.

These are just a few of the ways that you can help your customers save time. The productivity gains you help them achieve can be valued in a couple of ways. As with business to retail, your customers can use additional productive capacity (time savings) to generate more revenues. This is where the greatest value lies, for both you and your customers.

Generating More Revenue   There are four things you need to know to calculate the value of adding to your customers' revenue potential:

1. How much capacity you can add (2 percent, 5 percent, 20 percent)?
2. How many sales dollars can be generated with the additional capacity?
3. What gross profit percentage your customer typically earns (industry statistics are available in the reference sections of most public libraries)?
4. Whether there is adequate demand for your customers' offerings to convert the additional capacity to revenue?

If your customer is generating revenues of $500,000 a year and you increase that capacity by 5 percent, you've increased revenue potential by $25,000 ($500,000 × .05). At a profit margin of 30 percent, that's an additional $7,500 gross profit. Of course, your customer isn't going to share the full savings with you, but you can reasonably expect to get half. That affords your customer a 100 percent return the first year. Let's do the math:

Additional gross profit	$7,500
Less price premium paid to you	$3,750
Net profit improvement	$3,750
Profit improvement/price premium	100%

Who wouldn't want a 100 percent return the first year?

I'm sure that some of you are thinking, "My offering doesn't allow customers to increase production capacity! I sell a bolt that costs a few cents. It doesn't affect my customers' revenue potential." Really?

What happens to your customers' line when a part is just a little out of spec? The workers fiddle and jiggle until they find a way to make it work. While that's going on, the entire production line slows. How many more $20,000+ cars could have been produced if that three-cent bolt had fit right?

What about rework? The earlier in the process that your part is used, the more costly it becomes to replace *if* it isn't dependable. Let's say that your customer makes washing machines and your part is a bracket holding the motor in place. Once the washing machine is assembled, they run a test to make sure everything is working. Once in every 1,000 tests your bracket fails. That's 0.1 percent; not bad, right? Your customer has just foregone a sale of $400 (that's conservative) *and* suffered the cost of disassembling the machine, replacing the bracket and rebuilding the machine, easily tripling its labor cost on the machine.

As you can see, even the smallest components of a manufacturing/assembly operation can impact your customers' productivity – their ability to generate additional revenues. That's why the four things you need to know to calculate your price are the same whether you're selling a three-cent part or a $30,000 part.

So far we've talked only about the Cost of Goods Sold labor? What about the labor included in the Selling, General and Administrative Expenses? Can the same be said of it?

Certainly, helping a customer increase sales force productivity is going to help increase revenues, but by how much? Unlike the production side of things, where productivity increases typically translate into additional sales of *existing* products at *current* margins, sales productivity can open the door to more profitable revenue-generating opportunities.

A sales force with additional time can:

1. Increase sales of existing offerings at current margins.
2. Open new markets for their existing offerings.
3. Discover how customers' needs are evolving.
4. Find new uses for existing offerings.

Revenues and profit potential vary widely among these options. Increasing sales of existing offerings at current margins is the least profitable option. Being the first into a market affords your customer the ability to garner those huge innovator premiums we discussed earlier in the chapter. Yes, there are costs associated with creating market awareness, but the innovator premiums more than offset these costs.

A sales force that has time to visit with existing customers can learn how their customers' (your customers' customer) needs are changing. Advance knowledge is the key to gaining those innovator premiums and the profits they engender. The same premium profits are available when your customers' salespeople discover their customers using your offerings in ways they didn't envision.

Pharmaceutical companies find this all the time. Doctors, who prescribe a medication for its intended use, discover that patients experience other health benefits as well. Soon they're recommending the medication to patients who suffer these other maladies. Awareness of new uses for your customers' offerings can help them open new markets and get significantly higher prices than they're currently getting.

What's the value of each of these sales force productivity gains to your customers? Innovator premiums are available to your customer when they're first to open a new market, to introduce new offerings, or find alternative uses for existing offerings. Simply use the Innovator Formulae above to calculate your price.

A quick look at labor productivity in the General and Administrative areas will complete our analysis. Let's assume that your offering doesn't affect the productivity of the production or salespeople; it's limited to the General and Administrative folks. Let's also assume that your customers' General and Administrative Expenses are 20 percent of revenues and that you're able to help them increase General and Administrative productivity 10 percent.

A 10 percent productivity increase allows a customer generating $1 million in revenues to generate $1.1 million without adding any General and Administrative labor costs. So what are those productivity improvements worth to your customer? You're ahead of me aren't you? It's $20,000 ($100,000 additional revenue × 20 percent savings on General and Administrative labor costs).

Usually, the potential is much lower for increasing productivity in the General and Administrative area than the other areas of operation. That's because the General and Administrative expenses aren't directly related to sales. What's often overlooked is the impact that these folks can have on your customers.

When your finance person mandates more aggressive collection policies because cash flow has slowed, when payments to vendors are stretched to aid cash flow and delivery dates are missed, when your warehouse chief chooses not to send a truck out for a special delivery to a valued customer, when a customer's complaint is ignored, the potential for lost revenues is huge.

The value of general and admin productivity lies in the potential for lost revenues, not in cost savings. If your customer has a profit margin of 35 percent, losing $100,000 in sales would cost him or her $35,000 in gross profit. That's almost twice the $20,000 value of productivity enhancement we calculated a moment ago. It's an easy choice, isn't it?

Now that you have formulae for calculating value, let's get the customer to make these calculations. In Chapter 4, we'll show you how important it is to allow the customer to discover the value you provide.

Executive Summary

1. Some of the things customers value are speed, friendliness, integrity, dependability, convenience, image, service, innovation, and knowledgeable salespeople.

2. The above nine value attributes can be condensed down to three value propositions – image, innovation, and time savings.

3. Image buyers will pay five to ten times the lowest price alternative.

4. Innovation early adopters will pay two-and-a-half times what dependability buyers do and a whopping ten times what later adopters do.

5. Retail buyers will pay two to three times as much for recreation time as they will for the opportunity to make more money.

6. Business buyers want to know:
   - Can you help me increase revenues?
   - Can you increase work force productivity?
   - Can you help me cut costs?

7. Cutting costs is like going on a diet. It rarely produces lasting results.

8. Work force productivity has its greatest potential in increasing the productivity of your sales force, followed by increasing production labor productivity, with general and administrative labor productivity running a distant third.

CHAPTER 4

Customers' Delight: Discovering the Value

My three-year-old grandniece was jumping up and down when she suddenly stopped and said, "My hair's flopping!" I couldn't help but laugh at her excitement over her discovery.

Fortunately, the thrill of discovery doesn't wane with age. In October 2008, the news media reported that the bar-tailed godwit (a bird) flies 7,200 miles across the Pacific Ocean from Alaska to New Zealand *nonstop*. The trip takes more than eight days. It was a hot topic for days as people shared this amazing story with one another.

It's this excitement, this need to share a discovery, that you want your customers to experience. How do we accomplish this feat? Stop *telling* them how great your offerings are. Stop *telling* them what chumps they'd be for passing up this great opportunity. Instead, lead them through a journey of discovery.

The Power of Discovery

There's a reason why sales training courses teach salespeople how to ask questions. Actually, there are several reasons:

1. We don't like being told what to do. The desire for independence surfaces around age two and grows with age and experience.
2. We don't trust others very easily. Skepticism is our defense against those who would take advantage of us.
3. What we discover is more memorable. Plus, as with the godwit story above, it triggers a desire to share our discovery.

79

Asking customers and prospects questions that allow them to discover the value of your offerings bypasses all of these obstacles.[9]

Since you're not telling your prospects what to do, you avoid creating resistance to your ideas. Similarly, trust isn't an issue because they're validating their conclusions with their own experiences. And finally, their memory of the value of your offering is more vivid because they discovered it.

The key is to ask the right questions—questions that will allow your prospects to quantify the value of your offerings. If you tell them what that value is, you'll trigger their skepticism and their resentment at being told. If, however, you ask them questions that allow them to calculate the value, they'll validate the value with their own experiences. So what are these questions? How do we tap the power of discovery?

Before we can answer these questions, you need to know two things about your prospects. You need to know:

1. What they value – image, innovation, time-savings.
2. The degree of interest they have in that value proposition.

Just these two bits of information will help you determine quickly whether the person with whom you're talking is or is not an ideal prospect. Let's take a moment to refresh our memories. An ideal prospect is someone who values what you offer enough to pay a premium to get it.

How do you gather this information? Interestingly, it's simpler than you think. The answer to question #1, what do they value, can often be discerned within the first two minutes of the sales call. Here's how.

What Your Prospect Values

Imagine that you've just entered your prospect's office and exchanged greetings. The next words out of his mouth are, "What have you got for me?" That's all you need to hear to know what's most important to him. Time! This guy's all business. He doesn't have a moment to waste.

Let's contrast that with the person who asks about your weekend, comments on the weather, or regales you with a report of his kid's soccer game. This person values image and the personal service it portends. Quickly moving the conversation to business will turn him off. If the person asks "What's new and exciting?" or repeatedly interrupts your conversation to tell you about a new book, studies, products, or scientific discoveries, he values innovation. This is his hot button - the thing that will capture and retain his interest during the sales call.

Armed with these insights, you're able to determine whether or not the individual has the potential to be a good customer for you. Why is that important?

If your offering's *primary* value is image, time and innovation buyers aren't going to have much interest. If you do make the sale, it's likely that you lowered your price or made some concessions to get it. People aren't willing to part with their money unless they get something they really want or they get an incredible bargain. In Chapter 1, we saw numerous examples of how costly those "bargains" can be for you and your customers.

Back to our question: why is it important to know whether your prospect values what you offer? The cost of selling to the wrong buyer can be incredibly high, well beyond the costs outlined in Chapter 1. The cost is directly proportionate to the level of buyer interest. In the following paragraphs you'll discover what those costs are and how expensive they can be. Let's see what those costs are for each level of buyer interest.

The Degree of Interest

What interest does your prospect have? What impact does interest have on the value of the sale you're making? Indeed, what costs might you incur if you make sales to people who aren't really interested in your offerings? These are the questions we'll answer as we explore customers who have little or no interest, some interest, or genuine interest in you're offerings.

Little or No Interest

The advice I'm about to give goes against almost every salesperson's nature. If the prospect places little or no value on what you offer, walk away. The reasons are evident in the following example.

Let's say that you're an image buyer and the salesperson sitting across from you is touting time savings. While you like to save time, it's not as important as getting exceptional personal service or personal recognition. The salesperson senses this and gradually sweetens the deal to entice you to buy. It could be a discount, quicker delivery, or better payment terms. Regardless, she breaks down your resistance and you buy. What happens next?

You find that your interest wanes quickly. Buyer's remorse sets in. Yes, you got a good deal, but it's not really what you want. What do you do? You might:

- Return the item and ask for a refund.
- Ask for further concessions when a refund isn't available.
- Tell your friends that this wasn't as good a deal as you thought.
- Blame the salesperson for having mislead you.
- All of the above.

At this point I'm going to ask you to switch hats for a moment and look at the scenario above from the sellers' standpoint. Is there a winning scenario for the salesperson or her company in this list?

More importantly, what's the likelihood of being able to make another sale to this person in the future? *Nada!* Imagine what it would be like to have a new offering, one that's just right for this customer, only to realize that she won't do business with you again because you sold her something she didn't want. Imagine the frustration you'll feel as you realize just how expensive that earlier sale really was.

I'm sure that some of you are thinking, "I can't give up that quickly. It's possible that the prospect really doesn't know she wants." I agree. Yesterday, I was in a sales call where the prospect had a general idea of what he wanted to achieve, but not a clear goal. When I explained to him what was available, he found a concept he liked and bought on the spot. That's different than the situation in which he has little or no interest in my offering. Experienced salespeople know the difference.

The question is, "What do you do when, in those early minutes of the meeting, you discern that the buyer doesn't value what you have to offer?" Obviously you want to leave the door open for future business.

The most effective language I've discovered is, "I'm not sure that (my offering) is right for you." I know that some experienced salespeople use this "take away" or "take back" technique to engage a reluctant buyer and increase the likelihood of making the sale. My experience is that this is a misuse of a powerful tool that has ugly consequences. The consequences were listed above – refund requests, requests for additional concessions, derogatory comments about the company and offering, claims of unethical sales practices (hmm, could this be true?).

The power of the language, "I'm not sure that (my offering) is right for you," lies in its integrity. You're being honest with your prospect. You're demonstrating a genuine desire to see that the prospect gets what he or she wants instead of what you have to offer. This simple technique has many benefits. You gain:

- Credibility – prospects know that you're honest.
- A reputation for caring.
- People on the street touting you as one of the most honest, caring individuals they've ever met.
- People looking for opportunities to refer you because you took such good care of them. They want to repay your kindness.
- A stellar reputation for your company, making it easier for other salespeople in your organization to get introductions and make sales.

You avoid:

- The hassle of dealing with an unhappy customer.
- Losing revenues you could have generated by seeing more prospects instead of trying to satisfy an unhappy customer.
- Losing revenues due to your unhappy customer's complaints to family, friends, and business associates.
- Explaining to your good customers why they didn't get as good a deal as this unhappy customer did or, worse yet, reducing your price to your good customers to retain them.
- A reputation for caring more about the sale than the customer, which seriously diminishes your revenue potential.

In addition to gaining a reputation for being honest and caring, you demonstrate confidence in yourself and your offering, which leaves the prospect thinking, "If I ever need (what you offer), I'm going to call (you)."

Contrary to popular opinion, these memories are not short lived. People remember this type of kindness for years. If you doubt that, take a peek at Robert Cialdini's book, *Influence: Science and Practice.*[10]

Professor Cialdini relates the story of the gift of financial aid from Ethiopia to Mexico in 1985. Why would a struggling country like Ethiopia give financial aid to Mexico? In 1935, Mexico sent aid when Ethiopia was invaded by Italy. That memory lasted fifty *years.*

We do not forget people who treat us well, who place our needs ahead of their own. Nothing conveys the message that you care more clearly than walking away from a sale (commission) to make sure that the customer is well served.

The best approach for dealing with prospects who have little or no interest in what you offer is to say, "I don't think this . . . is right for you." Everyone wins – you, your prospect, and your company. Is the approach different for prospects who have at least a passing interest in what you have to sell?

Some Interest

Again, the odds are against you. While the prospect might not suffer the same degree of disappointment in your offering as the person with little or no interest, he is still not going to be satisfied with your offering. Here's the question you should be asking, "Is the potential gain from this sale worth the risk?"

You've already seen the risks. We discussed them earlier in the "little or no interest" section. These risks don't go away, nor do the costs associated with them. You've also seen what can be gained when you walk away from someone who is not your ideal prospect.

The most successful salespeople I know regularly walk away from prospects who aren't right for them. They know that the benefits they gain by walking away far outweigh the cost of one lost sale. They know that it takes longer to make a sale to a prospect who isn't interested. They know that the prospect isn't likely to be happy with the purchase. They know how much time and energy it takes to try to satisfy an unhappy customer and how futile that effort is. Instead of wasting huge amounts of time selling to the wrong prospects, they invest their time in finding people who value what they offer.

These salespeople make more money on each sale because their prospects *want* what they offer. They don't have to make as many sales to enjoy the lifestyle they desire. Yet they often make many more sales than their counterparts. This is the value of knowing who your ideal customer is and how to walk away when a prospect doesn't fit that mold.

We're not quite finished yet. There are factors to consider even within the realm of your ideal customer.

Genuine Interest

You know that you're with the right prospect when your offering's value proposition is:

- Time savings, and your prospect wants to get down to business quickly.
- Image, and your prospect wants to get to know you personally before doing business with you.
- Innovation, when the conversation centers around the latest or greatest.

This is where the real money is to be made.

Yet, even within this treasured realm, we find varying degrees of buyer interest. Each degree carries a different price premium. It's your job to determine where on the scale this prospect is so that you can maximize the potential of the sale. Let's take a look at how we accomplish this for each of our value propositions: time savings, image, and innovation.

Your Ideal Prospect's Interest

In the following sections we're going to explore ways to gauge your prospect's interest in image, innovation, and time savings. Let's begin our exploration with image.

Image

For your convenience, Table 4-1 summarizes the image premium multiples identified in the pricing formulae created in Chapter 3. These multiples will help us identify your prospect's interest in image.

As you can see, image premiums vary widely; clothing's range of 2× to 10× the least expensive offering encompasses all the other ranges. To help us determine the value image has to a prospect, we can use the following questions:

1. What clothing is he wearing? Is it Tommy Bahama (Nordstrom) or St. John's Bay (JCPenney)?
2. Where does she live? Everyone who has lived in a community for any length of time knows where the "high-rent" districts are, which areas the middle class inhabit, and where people who are struggling live. Prospects that live in prestige communities are at the top of the image premium range. The middle class is going to be at the middle or low end of the scale.
3. What car does your prospect drive? Is it a luxury or performance automobile? Is it that dependable Toyota Camry or Honda Accord? Is it a 12-year-old jalopy sorely in need of a new paint job?
4. In Table 3-1, "Value Attribute/Benefit Relationship," we saw that friendliness and name recognition are essential elements of image. How far does your prospect drive for name recognition, for exceptional service, to get the image he or she desires?
5. We also saw a link between innovation and image in Table 3-1. Some people buy innovation for the delight of experiencing new things, others buy it for the image it conveys. Which reason drives your prospect's innovation purchases?

Table 4-1. Image Price Premiums from Chapter 3

Reference	Item Purchased	Price Multiples	Premium %
Table 3-2	Clothing	2× to 10×	100% to 900%
Table 3-5	Automobiles	5.8× to 7.2×	480% to 620%
Table 3-6	Home Theaters	4.2× to 5.42×	320% to 442%

6. If your business takes you into your prospect's home, how is it decorated? Does it have a local flea market or professional designer ambiance?

7. If your sales call occurs in the prospect's office, how is the reception area decorated? How are the employees dressed? What's their demeanor? Does their Web site convey the same image as the reception area? What image does their marketing material convey? What image do they convey in published information (articles, advertising, infomercials)?

8. If you're selling business to business, what's your prospect's value proposition to their customers? Are they selling image, innovation, or time savings? As we saw in Chapter 2, value buyers become value sellers and price buyers sell price. The same is true for the nine value propositions identified in Table 3-1: speed, friendliness, integrity, dependability, convenience, image, service, innovation, and knowledgeable salespeople. Sellers emphasize what's important to them.

The key is to determine which of these indicators offers the best insight into your prospect's interest in image. If you're selling in a retail outlet, you may not be able to see what mode of transportation got the buyer to your shop, but you can tell what he or she is wearing.

If that doesn't work, steer the conversation to high school sports. If he has kids in that age range, he is almost certain to tell you how his kid's team is doing? Knowing his kid's school gives you a good idea of where he lives.

Is the buyer too young or too old to have kids? No problem. Reference upcoming events and see which interest him. If his interest is the symphony, you have an image-conscious buyer. Not so much so when he's headed to the monster truck show.

If automobiles are a good indicator of your prospects' interest in image, keep a car magazine handy—preferably one that has luxury or performance cars on the cover. Even though you can't see what mode of transport the prospect used to get to your store, the magazine will often elicit questions about your interest in cars. Of course, you'd be rude not to ask about his preferences. If the questions show a real interest in image cars, wonderful! If not, try anther approach.

You might also talk about an experience you had as a buyer in which you got exceptional service. Tell the buyer how far you have to travel; then let them know that it's worth the travel time. She'll likely regale you with a similar story. Their story provides you with the information you need to know what she's willing to do for friendliness, name recognition, and exceptional service.

If innovation is an important element of image for your buyers, what other innovations do they buy? What kind of price premiums do they pay for those innovations? You already know what these premiums are from your research in creating your pricing formulae. Don't hesitate to state that the price premiums are high, then add, "but it's worth it!"

When visiting your prospect's home, compliment the décor. Ask where you could find a similar piece. She's happy to share that information, especially when image is involved. Again, you'll have a sense for the price premium paid based on your earlier research.

Similarly, in the business world, compliment the prospect on the reception décor and the image it presents. He'll regale you with his perception of the importance of image. He'll also give you a sense for how important it is to his customers as well as what form that image takes – friendliness, name recognition, innovation. This information not only helps you frame your presentation, but helps you ascertain the level of premium the prospect is willing to pay. He's not likely to pay a higher premium than his customers are willing to pay.

When all else fails, don't be afraid to use the direct approach. Here's a sample script: "Different people value different things. What's most important to you when making this type of purchase?" If he or she struggles to answer your question, help out. Ask, "Is it friendliness? High-quality, name-brand merchandise? Innovation? Service after the sale?" Tell the prospect that this information is essential so that you can help her make an informed decision.

Many prospects will say that they value all of the above. Don't accept that answer. It's important to get them to commit to the one thing that's most important to them. An approach that works well is:

1. Acknowledge that all of the above are valuable.
2. Let them know that you want to make sure that they get what they really want.

3. Remind them that your ability to help them depends on your understanding of what's most important to them.
4. Make them choose; get them to narrow it down to, at most, two value attributes.

If you're not quite sure how to make them choose, ask them again, "Is it friendliness? High-quality, name-brand merchandise? Innovation? Service after the sale?" Then be quiet. Allow the silence to hang. Since many people are uncomfortable with silence, it's a subtle way to get them to answer your question.

Don't succumb to the silence yourself. The silence will be uncomfortable for you, too. Just remember, the one who speaks first relinquishes control. If you speak first, your prospect won't feel compelled to answer. If your prospect speaks first, you'll get your answer.

Now that you know what's truly important to them, you know what price premiums are available to you. If they're JCPenney buyers, your potential premium is roughly twice that of WalMart. If they're Nordstrom buyers, your potential premium rises to eight to ten times the WalMart price. You can make similar determinations when you know what they drive, where they go to decorate their homes, where they live, and so on.

The final step in the process is to get them to discover how much they value what you're offering. You accomplish them by helping them remember the premiums they paid for other image purchases with a similar price point.

You can tap these memories by asking, "How does it make you feel when you're wearing that beautiful designer dress or the Tony Bahama shirt? When you're driving your Mercedes, what feeling do you get? Do you feel that you've arrived; that you're the best in your field? What experience does your Bose sound system provide? What does that incredible sound quality do for you? What's it feel like when your friends seek your advice about new technology?"

These are not information gathering questions. Frankly, you don't care what the answer is. Your goal is to get them to experience the emotional high these image purchases provide.

The mind is a marvelous creation. It not only recalls prior experiences, but it allows you to *feel* the same emotions you felt at the time of the experience *with the same intensity*. It's this ability to relive the experience, to enjoy experiences over and over again, that drives us to repeat certain behaviors and avoid those with the opposite emotional impact. Remind your prospects of the joy they get from their image purchases. When they compare the emotional high they get against the price premium you're asking, it's a no-brainer. They're going to buy. Why wouldn't they? You've:

1. Done your homework; you know what price premiums people pay for similar offerings and priced your offerings accordingly.
2. Discovered what's important to your prospects and determined that your offering meets their needs.
3. Gained credibility with the buyers through your genuine desire to see that they get what they really want.
4. Allowed them discover the value of what you offer by helping them enjoy the emotional rush they get from their favorite activities.

Let's turn our attention to innovation for innovation's sake to see how we can help your prospects see the value of your innovation.

Innovation

Let's begin by refreshing our memories about the premiums that are available, as shown in Table 4-2:

Most of our discussions about innovation have centered on technology because it's the easiest to visualize. I fall into the dependability buyer category when it comes to technology. I don't enjoy spending time discovering software or hardware capabilities. I want to buy the tool that

Table 4-2. Innovation Price Premiums

Entry Into Market	Multiple Paid	Premium %
Early adopter	10× to 12× late adopter	900% to 1100%
Dependability buyer	4× to 5× late adopter	300% to 400%
Late adopter	0	0

fits the job, employ as little time as possible learning how to use it, and quickly move to the task at hand.

That doesn't mean that I'm not an innovation buyer. I'm just not an innovation buyer when it comes to technology. When I hear about concepts such as those discussed in the following books, I can't wait to discover the brilliant insights they afford:

- James Gleick's *Chaos: Making a New Science*
- Jim Collins' *Good to Great*
- Joseph Badaracco, Jr.'s *Leading Quietly*
- Robert Cialdini's *Influence: Science and Practice*

I'm so passionate about innovative ideas that my car has an autopilot setting for the bookstore. Here are some other ways innovation presents itself.

Doctors become innovators when they discover a pattern of unintended benefits that their patients experience when using a drug. Their keen observations become innovation.

Six Sigma and Lean Manufacturing have dramatically improved manufacturing productivity by streamlining processes, yet rarely do they involve new "technology." The innovation lies in knowing how to arrange a shop floor, the inventory needed, and identifying where in the system most of the failures occur.

The same can be said for your offerings. I'm confident that some of your customers are using your offerings in ways you didn't intend or are seeing value that you haven't imagined. Very early in my consulting work I had a number of clients tell me, "One of the things I really value about your service is the discipline it brings into my life."

I never did, and still don't, view myself as a disciplinarian. Yet the approach I use incorporates the things my clients need to help them stay focused on what's most important to their success. Hence, I add discipline to their lives. Pay attention to what your customers tell you and you, too, will see innovative ways to present your offerings.

Now that we understand that innovation takes many forms, how do we go about getting prospects to discover the value of innovation? The approach is similar to that employed in image. We need to get to the emotional high the prospects gets from innovation.

If their interest is in technology, why does it hold such appeal for them? Is it because they are innovators by nature and want to see how they can use others' innovations to spark their own innovations? Do they view innovation as an image enhancer, a way of demonstrating that they're on leading edge in their field? Is it a way to "Wow!" friends and colleagues who are less adventuresome or, like me, less patient with the quirkiness of new technology? Have they been one of those fortunate few who have retained their childhood curiosity?

To help you discover the answers to these questions, I'm going to do something a little different. I'm going to ask you to rate the four alternatives cited above in terms of their value to prospective buyers. We'll use a scale of 1 to 4, with 1 being the highest value the customer will gain and 4 being the lowest value. Here are alternatives; simply rank them 1 to 4:

_____   Spark innovation in their own offerings
_____   Image enhancement
_____   Wow friends and colleagues
_____   Childlike curiosity

Let me guess! You rated spark innovation as #1 and image enhancement as #2. Wowing friends and childlike curiosity are a toss up for numbers 3 and 4. Am I right? More importantly, what was the basis for my guesses?

As adults, we rely heavily on logic. We believe that emotions get in our way. That's why we see little value in emotions. Adults look at the alternatives and say that *logically* we should want to spark innovations in our own offerings because we know that innovation carries a high price premium. Our second *logical* choice is to want to enhance our image. We know that people like to do business with successful people. If we present the image of being successful, more people will want to do business with us.

Wowing friends and colleagues is fun, as are those rare moments when the child in us surfaces. They are, however, childish endeavors not worthy of our roles as responsible adults, parents, and providers. Therefore, logic would suggest, they have little value.

The reality is that it's the emotional aspect of our offerings that carry the greatest value. The greatest value in innovation is the thrill of discovery. It lies in that childhood curiosity; that three-year-old in us who realizes that our hair flops when we jump up and down. That's where the great value lies.

The second greatest value is in wowing friends and colleagues. We like the fact that they admire our adventurous nature, our childlike curiosity. We enjoy being viewed as someone on the cutting edge. We love having our friends come to us asking what works and what to avoid. The psychic rewards are "priceless."

The third greatest value lies in image. Early adopters of innovation are seen as leaders in their field. It's one of the reasons they gain the respect and admiration of others. What's that worth? In Chapter 1, we noted that the value of an "A" player is about 20 percent higher than a "B" player. If being an early adopter enhances that "A" image, then it has the potential to help boost your prospects' compensation by 20 percent. If they're making $50,000 a year, the potential value is $10,000 a year. At $100,000 a year, the value grows to $20,000 a year. Help your prospects make these comparisons, and you'll find that price is not an issue.

Another way of looking at a leader's value is by the number of people she manages. The greater number of people she manages, the more valuable she becomes. If your innovation has the potential to advance your prospect's career, to enable her to move up the organization chart, it becomes even more valuable.

The least valuable, although still significantly valuable, aspect of innovation is in its use in creating other innovations. Despite the huge price premiums available for innovation and the impact innovations have on our bottom line, few people view making money as their primary motivation in life. If money was the primary motivator, we'd all be billionaires. We focus on what we want most in life.

People who enjoy a great family life do so because that's what they want most in life and that's where they focus their attention. Those who want a successful career focus their attention on their work and enjoy great career success while sometimes losing family and friends in the process. Those who value recreation above all else will find ways to generate just enough money to enjoy their real interest in life – travel, hunting, fishing, shopping, crafts, or spending time with friends.

Armed with this knowledge, we can help the prospect discover the full extent of value that innovation has. If prospects demonstrate natural, childlike curiosity, relate a discovery you made that wowed you. Allow them to return the favor; allow them to describe discoveries they made. Then ask them to visualize that same feeling with your offering. These people will pay the highest premium for your offerings because they get the greatest emotional bang for the buck.

If your prospects also enjoy wowing friends, remind them of how good it feels to be admired by and sought out by friends who want the benefit of their experience. Help them relive prior experiences so that they can enjoy that admiration again. Help them see how they'll enjoy that experience again with your offering. Finally, use the stories they've told you about other innovative offerings they've purchased to remind them of the premiums they paid, the joy those offerings provided, and why the joy outweighed the premium. Assuming that your premium is in line with premiums paid for your price point, your price will seem insignificant in light of the joy and satisfaction they get from both their childhood curiosity and the admiration of their friends.

You see where I'm headed, don't you? If there is career advancement to be gained from enhancing their image or bottom line profits to be gained from adapting the innovations of others, it's a bonus! Don't hesitate to use it. When your prospects see that your offering can not only satisfy their natural curiosity, gain the admiration of friends and colleagues, and also enhance their career with all of the financial perks that accompany career advancement, the premium you're charging becomes even less significant.

The same is true for business owners. When your prospects discover the potential bottom line improvement they can gain on top of the wow and admiration factors, your price will seem like a bargain.

Remember, none of this works if you *tell* the prospect these advantages. You'll enjoy greater success when you:

- Ask the questions outlined above.
- Use examples to get them to remember how they felt in a similar situation.

- Allow them to relate their experiences back to you, then ask them to view your offering in the same light.

That's how you help them discover the value of innovation on their own.

Let's turn our attention to time savings with the same goal in mind – helping your prospects see that the value of their time is greater than your premium.

Time Savings

Once again, we'll analyze retail and business prospects separately since the alternative uses of time, the value proposition for time savings, are different for each.

Retail Prospects

Our task is simpler with retail prospects because there are only two alternative uses of their time: earning more money and recreation. Table 4-3 shows the premiums for each.

We've already discussed the fact that many people place a greater value on recreation time than on making more money. For those who prefer making money over taking time off, it's a fairly straightforward set of questions and calculations:

- How do you like to use your time off?
- It sounds like you enjoy that (money-making activity) even more than your regular job. Are you going into business for yourself?
- There certainly seems to be a market for (money-making activity). Is the potential as great as it appears?

Table 4-3. Time Savings Premiums for Retail Prospects

Alternative Use of Time	Comparison Base	Multiple
Earn more money	Customers' hourly pay rate	1×, no premium paid
Recreation	Customers' hourly pay rate	2× to 3×

You've probably noticed that I'm once again targeting their emotions. The more strongly your prospects believe that they can significantly enhance their income using your offering, the more valuable it becomes. Your premium pales as their income potential rises.

If prospects prefer recreation to making more money, find out how they spend their time off. Get a sense for what various types of recreation cost. What does it cost for someone who loves baking, chili, or BBQ to enter contests? What travel and lodging costs are involved? The same can be asked of fishing, hunting, shopping trips to Chicago's miracle mile, or, better yet, to Milan, Italy.

The more you know about various types of recreation, the levels of interest (participation), and cost of each, the greater your odds of getting a significant premium for your offerings. A shopping trip to Milan indicates a higher premium potential than one to Chicago (assuming you live in the United States).

Once you get a sense for the premiums your prospects pay, frame your offerings in light of those premiums. If your prospect spends $25,000 to $50,000 for a bass boat, spends $3.00 to $4.00 a gallon for gas to tow it, similar gas prices to race around the lake locating the best fishing spots, pays tournament entry fees, and spends a night or two in a local motel, what are the odds that your premium is going to seem unreasonable?

The key is to ask them questions that allow them to make these comparisons on their own. Questions like:

- How do you like to spend your time off?
- How often do you (recreation activity)?
- Where's the best place to for (recreation activity)?
- If you had the opportunity, would you move there?

These questions are designed to help the prospect discover just how important this activity is to them. Now it's a matter of helping them discover how much time they'll save with your offering so that they can spend more time doing what they really love to do. You've just helped them discover the value of your offering. It's also given you a good indication of how much premium they'll pay to enjoy these activities.

How does this differ from business to business sales? Let's take a look.

Business Prospects

Our task here is more complex because we're dealing not only with the business owners' time, but staff time as well. Table 4-4 shows the premiums associated with time savings in the major operating areas most companies encompass.

In business-to-business situations, it's all about making money. Or is it? Again, there are a variety of reasons why people want more money. They want money:

- For the freedom it affords them.
- To demonstrate how good they are at what they do.

Table 4-4. Premiums Associated with Alternative Uses of Time for Business Prospects

Alternative Use of Time	Value of Alternative Use of Time
Sales force	Selling more of your existing offerings = increased revenue potential × gross profit on existing offerings
	Selling to previously untapped markets = increased revenue potential × 120% to 150% of existing gross profit of existing offerings
	Finding ways for your company to fill unfilled customer needs = innovation premiums
Production staff	Increased revenue potential × gross profit on existing offerings
General and administrative staff	Increased revenue potential × the productivity improvement

- To provide a secure financial future for their spouses and kids.
- To have more time for their hobbies.
- For philanthropic purposes.
- To leave a legacy in the form of a company that survives them.

These are the real driving forces behind the desire to make money. Your goal is to help them understand their true motivation. The psychic rewards of using money for the purposes outlined above exceed, by far, the monetary results achieved.

That doesn't mean that you should ignore the monetary value. When you ask them:

- Do you want to increase revenues?
- Do you want to increase sales force productivity?
- What would an increase in production productivity add to your bottom line?
- What would an increase in admin productivity do for your bottom line?

The follow up questions are the same ones that we asked when we created the formulae for quantifying value:

- Would the increase in revenues come from a price increase? If so, what kind of premium can we get? What will that do for your bottom line?'
- If you increase unit sales within existing markets, what margin can you expect? How many more units can you sell? What will that do for your bottom line?
- Are you entering a previously untapped market? What kind of premium exists for innovation in your industry? How many units can you sell? What marketing and sales costs would you incur to generate those sales? What impact will that have on your bottom line?
- If you increase the productivity of your sales force, where do you expect them to devote their energies? Is market demand ade-

quate to make it worthwhile to increase capacity? If so, what bottom line improvement can you expect?

- Your production department's productivity needs a boost. Why? What will you gain in revenue potential? Is there adequate demand to utilize the additional capacity you're creating? If so, what bottom line impact will it have? If not, how will you utilize the additional capacity? What value does that have?
- Similar questions can be asked for administrative productivity. Will the time saved just eliminate costs or will it be utilized to enhance customer satisfaction? If the goal is to improve the customer experience, how valuable is that to the customer? What kind of premium could you get for the additional satisfaction? What will that add to the bottom line?

The answers to these questions lay a strong foundation for the premiums you charge when you help a businesses save time. Yet, the greatest value lies in the business owners' reason for wanting to make money. Help them discover the combined value – bottom line impact and achievement of their personal goals – and you'll have no problem getting a premium for your offerings.

As you can see, your prospects can take many paths to discover the incredible value your offerings afford. Help them discover:

- The path that has the greatest value for them.
- The full range of value they can achieve.
- That your offering is like other purchases they've enjoyed.
- That your premium isn't any higher than those other purchases.
- The joy of owning what you're selling.

In doing so, you allow them come to the realization that your premium is, indeed, small in relation to the value they're getting. Do this well, and you'll reap the benefits you so richly deserve. You'll be compensated well for the value that you provide.

It's time to turn our attention to another tool for getting premium pricing – bundling. On to Chapter 5!

Executive Summary

1. People resist being told things; they'd much rather figure them out on their own. That's why it's essential that you lead them on a journey of discovery – discovery of the value you provide and the joy it affords.
2. Regardless of what value proposition you use, your prospects need to discover what they value and the intensity with which they value it. The higher the intensity, the greater the value.
3. You can typically get a sense for what a prospect values – image, innovation, or time savings - within the first two minutes of a sales call.
4. If your value proposition doesn't match the prospects' interests, exit quickly and gracefully.
5. Saying to a prospect, "I'm not sure that (my offering) is right for you?," when it's true, gains you tremendous respect and credibility and often leads to referrals.
6. When you're selling image, pay attention to details like what your prospects are wearing, where they live, what they're driving, and where their kids go to school. All of these are indicators of how important image is to them.
7. If you're selling innovation, remember that buyers will pay more to satisfy their childlike curiosity and wow their friends and colleagues than they will to enhance their income stream.
8. When selling time savings to the retail market, remember that buyers will typically pay two to three times more to get recreation time than they will for the opportunity to make more money.
9. If you're selling business to business, the real value of time savings doesn't lie in the ability to make more money, but in the psychic rewards in the use of that money.
10. Know what value proposition your business prospects use in selling to their customers. Sellers reflect their buying preferences. Knowing what your prospect values helps you determine whether or not they're likely to be interested in your offering.

CHAPTER 5

Icing on the Cake: Bundling for Greater Profits

When you saw the word "icing," what did it conjure up? Was it sinfully delicious dark chocolate on yellow cake? Tantalizing banana icing on banana cake? How about a silky cream cheese icing on carrot cake? Or was it the icing on Aunt Ethel's third cousin's grandniece's wedding cake that you swore ate half the enamel off your teeth with the first bite?

All of us enjoy a sweet deal, but just like icing on a cake it can be overdone. Bundling is a delicate blend of ingredients that:

- Sweetens the deal for your customers.
- Increases your average sale.
- Boosts your employees' productivity.
- Reduces your risks.

For those of you who may not be familiar with the term "bundling," a bundle is a group of products and/or services designed to make your offerings more attractive to your customers and more profitable for you. Bundling is the process of creating those groups of offerings.

What Bundling Can Do for Your Business

Before we embark on creating bundles and gathering ingredients for those bundles, let's see what bundling can do for your customers, your average sale, your employee's productivity, and you in minimizing the inevitable risks that you face. We'll start, as we always should, with your customers. How does bundling sweeten the deal for them?

Sweetens the Deal for Your Customers

First, bundling sweetens the deal for your customers. This is not achieved by adding more to the offering, but by helping your customers and prospects see your offering in a different light. It's achieved by making the customers aware of all the benefits they're already getting—benefits that they and you often overlook. As we'll see in examples later in this chapter, many existing offerings include benefits that neither buyers nor sellers recognize. For example, virtually every worthwhile offering includes convenience. By identifying and communicating the convenience your offering affords, you sweeten the deal for your customers *without* adding any new features or benefits to that offering.

As we saw in Chapter 1, adding features and benefits to your offering without raising prices simply drives up your cost. This practice is often the result of your desire to distinguish your offerings from those of your competitors. As we discovered, these enhancements often have little or no value to your customer, which means that all you've really accomplished is higher costs. Helping your customers see how sweet your deal already is helps you avoid these needless costs. Now you and your customer are both enjoying a sweet deal. The deal becomes even sweeter *for you* when you discover how bundling increases your average sale.

Increases Your Average Sale

Bundling to meet your customers' desires and needs allows you to increase your average sale. McDonald's knows that a significant number of its customers want more than just a sandwich. They want hash browns and a drink to go with that Egg McMuffin. So McDonald's makes it easy for its customers to get what they want by bundling all three into a meal. In doing so, McDonald's just increased the sale from roughly $2.30 to approximately $3.40, a whopping 48 percent increase in revenues. You, too, can experience average sale increases of 40 percent or more through bundling.

Some of you are thinking, "Okay, I get it. I can see how bundling would increase my average sale, but where's the productivity increase come in?"

Boosts Your Employees' Productivity

Imagine that you enter McDonald's and order an Egg McMuffin. The counterperson asks, "Do you want hash browns?" It takes you a few seconds, but you decide that yes, you want hash browns. You open your wallet as she asks, "Do you want something to drink?" You do, but do you want some caffeine to jump start your day or are you going healthy with orange juice? It takes a few seconds, but your guardian angel wins out and you go with the orange juice. "What size?" you're asked. Let's see, how thirsty are you? Actually, at this point you're tired of the inquisition and you decide on a medium. How long did that exchange take? Ten to twelve seconds? More?

Let's rewind the clock. You enter McDonald's to order breakfast. You glance at the display showing your options – sandwich or meal. You've faced with one question: "Am I hungry enough for a meal?" If you are, you've just spared yourself the remaining questions. Why? You know that you want the hash browns. You know that you want a drink and, because we're creatures of habit, you order the drink you typically have with breakfast. This bundling saves you, the customer, from answering these annoying questions. It also saves you time; the whole process of deciding meal or no meal and ordering only takes four seconds instead of a minimum of ten as in the previous example.

You're not the only one saving time, though, are you? That person behind the counter also saved six to eight seconds. That's one-and-a-half to two additional orders that person could take. That's the productivity McDonald's gains from bundling. Wouldn't you like to be able to improve your employees' productivity like that? It's available to you when you bundle your offerings. We're still not finished; bundling also helps you reduce your risk.

Reduces Your Risks

Staying with our McDonald's example, let's consider the folks in the back putting the orders together. If every order on the display screen includes three to four items, what are the odds that periodically these employees are going to pick up an item from one order and read it into another?

Let's contrast that with two options on that display screen—sandwich or meal? The odds of a mistake are reduced, which means that customer satisfaction and loyalty are increased, while waste, too, is reduced. Sweet! A sweet deal for you, and a sweet deal for your customers.

Now that you have a sense for the benefits bundling affords, let's figure out what ingredients are needed to create a great bundle.

Creating Bundles: Examples and Exercises

Each of the five examples that follow provides the background information you need to gain experience in bundling offerings. Don't be concerned that you don't have industry experience; often the lack of industry familiarity makes it easier to see bundling opportunities.

In each example you're going to be asked a series of questions that guide you through the bundling process. I encourage you to answer these questions before reviewing my answers. The only way to develop this skill, as with any skill, is through practice. These examples allow you to practice without risk. It's a lot cheaper to make mistakes in these exercises than when you're sitting in front of a prospect.

I'm *not* going to share actual numbers with you in these exercises for two reasons. One is that it would violate my confidentiality commitment to the clients I've served over the years. The other is that for people who struggle with math the numbers cloud the issue.

We'll begin with the horse trainer example we used in Chapter 1.

Horse Trainer Example
Here's the background information I promised:

- A strong bond exists between riders and their horses when they compete in hunter/jumper events. It's a sport that's dangerous for both. These competitors (rider and horse) must each trust that the other party has their welfare at heart.
- The trainer believed that the well-being of the horse was paramount. She didn't feel that depriving a horse of a blanket in winter because the owner hadn't paid for it made sense.
- Stables that provide board, but no training, offer an *à la carte* menu. There is a base price for feeding the horse and cleaning the stalls. Delivering medications, turning the horse out in an exercise area, providing fans and fly spray in the summer and blankets in the winter, etc., are considered extras; each carries a separate price tag.

- This trainer's reputation for training both horse and rider was renowned. Her students regularly brought home awards for their and their horses' performances.
- When customers wanted to enter a show (contest), they simply called the trainer and let her know. She made the reservations, handled the paperwork, made sure that all health certificates were available for inspection, transported the horse and tack to the show, took care of the horse and tack at the show, got the horse ready for competition, advised the rider during competition, and transported and resettled the horse back at her barn after the competition. These show services were billed separately from the boarding and training services.
- Other hunter/jumper horse trainers typically have separate charges for boarding, training, and show services.
- Place yourself in the role of this horse trainer and answer the following questions.

Space has been provided below each question so that you have room to record your responses. Later, I'll share my thoughts with you. Here are the questions:

1. How you would bundle these offerings?

2. Why did you choose to bundle them in that way?

3. What obstacles did you face in creating the bundle?

4. What benefits does the customer gain from your bundle? (*Hint:* Use the value propositions we discussed in Chapter 3.)

5. What questions might your bundle trigger when your customers and prospects compare your bundle with your competitors' offerings?

I hope that you took the time to do the exercise. Gaining experience in bundling the offerings in these examples will make bundling your offerings much easier and more effective. If you didn't complete the exercise, please do so *now*. You'll not only accelerate your learning, you'll enjoy greater success in creating your own bundles. Now for a glimpse at my answers. Here's what my client and I did:

1. What bundles did we create?

All of our bundles included boarding, training, and show services. Boarding was exactly the same for all bundles—the horse's health and welfare were paramount, so all bundles included everything that a horse might need to enjoy good health.

Training and show services were bundled based on frequency. Customers could contract for training lessons for themselves and their horses one, two, or three days a week. They also had the option of individual or group lessons—options designed to accommodate a variety of budgets.

Customers could choose to compete in one, two, four, or six shows a year. The flexibility of these bundles allowed customers to determine where to invest their money—in training, show services, or a combination of the two. It also gave them several budget levels from which to choose.

2. Why did we bundle in this way?

We recognized that boarding stables were not our competitors. Our ideal customer wants to win competitions. The boarding, while a necessary part of the horse's well-being, is not the primary reason that prospects and customers seek our services.

We also realized that our philosophy about horse care was dramatically different than that of the traditional boarding stable where the customer decided, via the *à la carte* menu, what care the horse received.

So we bundled the complete boarding care with the training. Customers could sign up for lessons once, twice, or three times a week. They also had the option of choosing group or individual lessons. Obviously, the individual lessons carried a higher price tag than the group lessons.

Further, we realized that the show services were problematic. The fees for the various contests varied widely from location to location. The cost of transport also depended upon locale.

Previously my client kept track of these costs and then billed the customer as part of a final accounting. This approach:

- Created a lot of paperwork for the trainer.
- Required the customer to spend time reviewing the invoice.
- Occasionally presented the customer with some unpleasant surprises.
- Required this trainer to front the cash for many of these costs.

We bundled the shows into the training and boarding packages, again, using frequency as our guide. The customer could sign up for one, two, four, or six shows a year. We used the cost of the highest entry fee, the greatest travel distance, and the popularity of the event to guide us in establishing a price per show. The price of the show was built into the package that the customer bought.

3. What obstacles did we face in creating these bundles?

Finding the right mix of show and training services. Customers aren't going to win without adequate training for themselves and their horses. Similarly, they can't win if they don't compete. Creating bundles that balanced customers' desire to win with the level of training necessary to help them achieve that goal was challenging.

4. What did customers gain from these bundles? They gained:
    a. A simplified decision-making process. There were options available to fit the budget of anyone serious about competing in hunter/jumper events.
    b. The knowledge their horses would get the best care.
    c. Convenience. They got one bill a month, and it was always for the same amount. They didn't have to spend time reviewing the invoice to see that they were only being charged

for services they requested as they would at a traditional boarding stable. They also avoided the hassle of analyzing itemized show expenses.

d. The ability to budget their costs. Again, one invoice every month for exactly the same amount allows customers to manage their budgets more effectively.

What I'd like you to notice is that we didn't add any new features to my client's offerings. Training, boarding, and show services were always a part of her offerings. Nor did we change the nature of these offerings. Her philosophies of horse care, training, and competitive advantage remained as they always were—top notch.

With that in mind, how did we manage to add so many valuable benefits to our customers? How did the simplified decision-making process, the horse's welfare, and the convenience of monthly budgeting/bill paying surface as valuable benefits for the customer? The answer may surprise you.

If you recall, in Chapter 3 we listed nine value attributes:

- Speed
- Friendliness
- Integrity
- Dependability
- Convenience
- Image
- Service
- Innovation
- Knowledgeable salespeople

These nine attributes were then condensed to three value calculations—image, innovation, and time savings. Sound familiar?

In bundling this horse trainer's services, we simply reversed the process. We took the image and time savings characteristics of her offerings and looked at the underlying value attributes that make up those two characteristics. Here's the thought process we went through.

Image is important to this horse trainer's customers. They want to be viewed as exceptional riders who have great respect for and take great care of their horses. The horse's health shows up in the sheen in the horse's coat, its solid musculature, and its stamina during the performance. The training for both horse and rider are evident in their performances during the show. As you can see, we simply took the image concept and exploded it to point out these various aspects (evidence) of image, knowing that these are things that are important to the owner.

Customers also wanted convenience (time savings). We provided that by keeping the monthly invoice exactly the same. A mere glance at the invoice would assure them that the invoice was correct. The fixed monthly fee allowed them to avoid having to scramble to come up with money to cover show costs. Why? These costs were included in the fixed monthly amount. Simplifying the budget and bill paying process saves the customer time because it was convenient.

I promised you, in the "Sweetens the Deal for Your Customers" section above that I would show you how to distinguish yourselves from your competitors *without adding new benefits*. This process of exploding the three value calculations back out to the value attributes is what allows you to accomplish that goal. This simple approach is one of the most powerful ways I've found for getting customers to see value that already exists— value that they, and you, often overlook.

5. Finally, I asked you to anticipate the questions this horse trainer's prospects and customers might have. Here are the questions my client anticipated and the responses we scripted:

Q. I'm just looking for a place to board my horse. What do you charge?

A. I'm sorry, but I'm not sure that we're the right service for you. We specialize in hunter/jumper training. Boarding is simply an accommodation for our training customers. I can give you the names of reputable stables in the area that specialize in boarding.

Q. I want to become a better rider. How much do you charge for lessons?

A. I'm sorry, but I'm not sure that we're the right service for you. We specialize in training horses and riders who want to compete in hunter/jumper events. Is that what you're interested in? If not, I can give you the names of some very good trainers who can help you become a better rider.

Q. I really like the package that includes three private lessons a week for me and my horse and three shows a year. I'm just not sure I can afford it.

A. I certainly understand that. We all have budget constraints. That's why we offer a variety of packages to meet any budget. Why don't we start out with a smaller package and see whether you and your horse need private lessons three times a week or whether you can allocate more of your budget to the shows?

The full list of questions we anticipated is more extensive than the examples outlined above. The questions above are, however, adequate for you to gain an understanding of the things you need to do in a sales call to deal with the questions and objections your customers have. Before I share the thoughts behind our answers, I encourage you to assess both the questions and answers for yourself. In particular, for each of the questions, what was the goal of our response? Record your response in the space provided. Here are the questions again:

Q. I'm just looking for a place to board my horse. What do you charge?

Q. I want to become a better rider. How much do you charge for lessons?

Q. I really like the package that includes three private lessons a week for me and my horse and three shows a year. I'm just not sure I can afford it.

Just a reminder that you become more proficient as you gain experience. Please use these exercises as a way to develop that proficiency.

There's no risk, no cost, associated with being wrong here. That's not true when you're in the field talking to a prospect or customer. Take full advantage of the risk-free opportunity for skill development this book affords.

Now that you've completed the exercises, let's compare notes. What message(s) were we sending with our answer to the question "I'm just looking for a place to board my horse. What do you charge?"

Our response is designed to communicate clearly who our ideal customer is. We left the door open for the prospect to inquire more about the hunter/jumper training, but we left no doubt that we weren't in the business of just boarding horses. Finally, we referred the customer to reputable stables in the area that would meet their needs. This trilogy of communiqués saves the prospect time and demonstrates our confidence in both our ability to provide exceptional value and the existence of a market for that value, as well as a desire to help prospects get what they want.

Do you think that this prospect might refer others to my client? You bet they will. Why? My client didn't waste the prospect's time, didn't denigrate his interest in just boarding their horse, and helped him find resources to fit their needs.

What message or messages were we sending with our answer to the second question, "I want to become a better rider. How much do you charge for lessons?"

Again, we clearly communicated who our ideal customer is, left the door open for the prospect to express an interest in our offerings, and referred the prospect to reputable trainers who would meet their needs.

We explained that we don't provide all types of training, just hunter/jumper training and only for people who want to compete. We check their interest in that offering as well as learn more about what they're trying to accomplish. Then we use that information to complete the sale or refer them to someone who would be ideal for helping them achieve their goal. Prospects get the same benefits as from the response to the first question—time savings, respect for their desires, and a way to get them satisfied. And in the end, my client gained another potential referral source.

Will we see the same benefits from the response to our third question? The question was, "I really like the package that includes three private lessons a week for me and my horse and three shows a year. I'm just not sure I can afford it."

In this instance, we already know that we have an interested buyer. He or she is just checking to see whether a better deal is available. Our response, in essence, says:

- What we offer is valuable and the price isn't negotiable. In other words, the price isn't coming down unless you're willing to give something up.
- We are confident in our business model. There are plenty of people willing to pay our price to get that value.
- We're willing to walk away from business that doesn't make sense for us. (Another statement of confidence.)
- We respect the fact that you have a budget, and we'll work with you to find an option that best suits your needs. We are not, however, creating a new option.
- The door is always open for you to choose another option in the future. You're not locked into the decision you make today. We realize that needs change, which is why we offer a variety of packages.

How would you feel if the person whose offerings you were considering treated you this way? I believe that most of us would agree that the confidence, clarity, candor, and caring included in these responses would cause us to want to do business with my client or, at least, refer business to her. These are the benefits you gain when you learn how to effectively bundle your offerings and script your responses for the various prospects you might encounter. Let's take a look at some more examples so that you can gain even more experience.

Clothing Purchase Example

You're a clothing retailer. You've had good success, but just can't seem to get to the next level of sales and profitability. A friend recently told you about bundling and said that there were six questions you need to answer to create profitable bundles. You've decided to give it a shot. Here are the questions for you to answer and the space to enter those answers:

1. What are some of the challenges shoppers face in buying clothing?

2. Can bundling help them overcome these challenges?

3. What could I bundle together to make life easier for my customers?

4. What benefits would they gain from these bundles?

5. What benefits would I, as the clothier, gain from these bundles?

6. What script(s) would I use to communicate these benefits to my customers?

Let's compare answers. By the way, this isn't a quiz. There aren't any right or wrong answers, just myriad approaches. I'm simply sharing some of my thoughts with you.

1. What are some of the challenges shoppers face in buying clothing?

   - A few of us are color blind; more of us have limited color memory—the color our mind conjures up isn't the actual color of the garment we own.
   - Some of us have no fashion sense.

- When buying for others, we use our style as a frame of reference even this often conflicts with the other person's style.
- We forget to make related purchases while in the store.
- We can't afford ten different outfits, so we need to mix and match components to create different looks.

2. Can bundling help customers overcome these challenges?

- Over the years, I've appreciated the displays that show me how different color combinations work. I typically buy shirts and ties at the same time I buy suits so that I don't have to remember what color the suit is or wear the suit back to the store to make sure that the shirts and ties will match. Bundling shirt and tie combinations with suits, shirt/sweater combinations, and shoes/handbags/accessories with the primary purchase can help those of us who are color challenged.
- Fashion sense seems like a fairly straightforward concept until you begin to consider generational differences. What I, at age 60, might consider fashionable is not the same thing that a 20-year-old is going to find fashionable. Then, there's body type. Vertical stripes can help a robust figure seem trimmer, but may make an already trim figure look emaciated. Bundling by age (this could be attitudinal age instead of chronological age; some of us feel and act younger than our years) and body type can help buyers make better choices for themselves.
- Buying for others is always a challenge, but establishing displays that focus buyers' attention on the individuality of styles can help. Let's consider bundling offerings for that recent graduate who needs to make a good first impression on the job; the 20-something party animals who can't wait to shed their drab workday image; the young mother who wants to remain stylish, but doesn't have a lot of time to find just the right outfit; the professional who wants to send the message "I've arrived"; and older buyers who want to maintain some semblance of current fashion sense, but don't have the body style to pull it off. These are very real challenges that people face when buying for others. Having bundles available that target different stages in life can be a tremendous help to those who choose to or must buy for others.

- Have you ever gotten home with a new pair of shoes, then realized that your hosiery was getting a little ragged? Have you ever bought a suit thinking that one of your ties would be perfect only to find that the colors aren't even close? Have you bought new shirts or blouses only to find that your slacks are more worn than you remembered? Wouldn't it be nice if somehow the store reminded you to consider those things *before* you got home? Bundling shoes and socks, shirts or blouses with slacks and skirts, and ties with suits can easily solve this problem for your customers.

3. What could I bundle together to make life easier for my customers?

    - Shirts and ties with suits.
    - Shoes and handbags, scarves, and other accessories.
    - Blouses, skirts, and jackets for multiple outfits.
    - Shirts and sweaters.
    - Shoes, hosiery, and belts.
    - Each of the above combinations for the various stages of life.
    - Each of the above combinations for various body styles.

4. What benefits would customers gain from these bundles?

    - Buyers will save time. Whether shopping for themselves or others, buyers will find what they want more quickly. They won't have to return as many purchases, and they'll save that frustrating trip to the store to buy what they forgot.
    - They'll be confident in their purchases because they're making color comparisons in the store rather than later guessing what will or won't work color-wise.
    - Buyers will be able to add more versatility and functionality to their wardrobes by mixing and matching.
    - Buyers who don't pay a great deal of attention to fashion will get a chance to see what current trends are in mixing and matching.

5. What benefits would I, as the clothier, gain from these bundles?

    - I would have the opportunity to increase my average sale. The customer who isn't quite sure whether he needs to replace some socks will probably buy a few pair just to be sure. The woman who needs three pieces to make six outfits for budget purposes will buy bundles that help her meet that goal. People who want to be true to the image of the person for whom they're buying will buy a set, especially if they think that person lacks fashion sense.

- My employees' productivity will go up because they will be generating more sales dollars per customer.
- I will reduce my return risk by creating bundles that produce the look my customers are seeking.

6. What script(s) would I use to communicate these benefits to my customers?

- If you love to shop and have the time, take your time and enjoy the experience, but if you're in a hurry and don't have a lot of time to figure out what works and what doesn't, we've created some stunning ensembles to fit your lifestyle.
- Buying for someone else? We know how challenging that can be, so we've arranged our store around different lifestyles and body styles to help you get just the right outfit for that special person.
- If you're like me (it's always good to let your customers see that you suffer the same challenges they do) and you don't remember colors well, don't take a chance that your shirts and ties match this new suit. Pick from any number of ensembles we have created to help convey your personal image and style.

Computer Example

You're Steve Jobs (don't you wish). Here's the situation you face:

1. Everyone who uses your computers raves about them. They won't use your competitor's product again unless they simply don't have a choice.
2. Your computer is one of the most stylish machines available.
3. You've solved some of the software availability problems by allowing your machines to run both your and your competitor's operating systems.

4. Your company is noted for innovation—not just for its computers, but for all of its offerings.
5. Despite all of these pluses, you still only have a small percentage of the computer market.

What can you do about it? Can bundling help you in this situation? Let's use our questions to see what you, Steve Jobs, could do to increase sales. Record your thoughts below beneath each question.

1. What are some of the challenges computer buyers face?

2. Can bundling help them overcome these challenges?

3. What could I bundle together to make life easier for my customers?

4. What benefits would they gain from these bundles?

5. What benefits would I gain from these bundles?

6. What script(s) would I use to communicate these benefits to my customers?

Here are some thoughts I had regarding these questions:

1. What are some of the challenges computer buyers face?
   - They don't understand the lingo. They wouldn't know a duo core processor if it bit them. Yet we're asking them to choose between a duo core and a quad core processor. They don't know how much memory they need, what megahertz speed they need, or what software will or will not run on your operating system.
   - The confusion outlined above causes buyers to forget, or overlook, what it is that they're really trying to accomplish with their computer. Lacking a clear goal for making the purchase, they often choose the wrong solution.
   - Many personal computer users would like to change to your computer, if for no other reason than to avoid the virus and spy attacks they experience with PCs. The problem is that they don't want to learn a new operating system. Either they don't feel that they have the time or they'd rather use their time in other ways.

2. Can bundling help them overcome these challenges?
   There are several options available to you:
   - Bundling according to budget limitations is one way. You could offer one model that has basic functionality, a second model with some bells and whistles, and the innovator's delight —the model that has every feature imaginable.
   - You could also bundle by stage of life:
     (a) You could have a version for small children that has age-appropriate games, movies, and music—all designed to tap into the child's natural curiosity and engender a love of learning.
     (b) Another version could target older students who have papers to write as well as a burning desire to stay connected with their friends. The Internet with its research capabilities and email and voice mail availability would be the essential elements of this package.
     (c) Business owners and career professionals have yet other needs. They need productivity tools including CRM (customer relationship management) software, mobile contact capabilities, performance measurement tools, etc.

(d) Grandparents want connectivity with their children and grandkids. Since travel has become more expensive and more of a hassle, being able to have video capabilities to see their families as well as speak with them is a real plus. This generation also enjoys creating family photo albums and sending pictures of places visited to friends and family, which triggers an interest in Photoshop and similar photo editing software.

3. What could I bundle together to make life easier for my customers?

   • We already have some ideas of what software to include for each stage of life. If we combine each of these with the three budget options mentioned above, we have something for almost every lifestyle.
   • Training could be added to help buyers make the transition from your competitor's operating system to yours easier and less painful.

4. What benefits would they gain from these bundles?

   • Buyers would find it much easier to decide which system is right for them. If I'm a grandparent who loves video and Photoshop capabilities, I may also value the larger screen because my eyesight isn't what it used to be. Combining these benefits into one bundle helps buyers save time.
   • Gift-giving is also easier. Parents and grandparents who believe strongly in early childhood education can purchase educational models for those preschoolers in their lives. This saves the giver time by simplifying the selection of the gift and minimizing the likelihood of its return.
   • Even though storage (disk space) and memory are both relatively inexpensive, buyers won't feel like they're paying for software that has little or no value to them because the software that's included is matched to their interests.
   • The look and feel of the computer can be tailored to the user's stage of life. You're already renowned for its designs. Why not take to one step further and create a separate look for each stage of life? It's an easy and inexpensive way to add an element of image to the offerings.

- The technology itself becomes inconsequential; it's the lifestyle needs that are addressed. The fact that buyers don't have to understand or, worse yet, make decisions based on technology saves them time.
- You already offer training once a week all year for about $100 a year. This inexpensive training minimizes buyer reluctance in shifting from PCs.

5. What benefits would I, Steve Jobs, gain from these bundles?

- Accelerated sales, because buyers are able to focus on their interests instead of the technology.
- Even higher premiums than you're currently getting, because the image component has been enhanced and the time savings dramatically increased.
- More frequent repeat sales, because buyers' needs change more quickly. A preschooler, whose learning is well ahead of his or her contemporaries, may ask for the student model much earlier than normal. That pattern is likely to continue as that student moves into business, the sciences, teaching, or other career pursuits. The earlier the transitions are made, the greater the potential number of computers you can sell.

6. What script(s) would I use to communicate these benefits to my customers?

- If I'm talking to a grandparent or parent interested in early education, I'm going to talk about how competitive the world is and how vital education will be to future success.
- If those grandparents don't share the aforementioned view of the world and can't afford to travel as often as they'd like to visit the kids and grandkids; I'm going to emphasize the videoconferencing capabilities of the system.
- A business person is going to be thrilled when I tell him that some of the most popular and effective productivity tools are already loaded on the system. I'll also mention that he is not as likely to be spammed, suffer virus attacks, or have people spy on him using my computer. I'd remind them how long the start up is on a personal computer because of the antivirus and spyware software.

- College students are going to appreciate the fact that I've focused their limited budget dollars on what's important to them. Connectivity with friends and family and Internet research capabilities.
- In all of these scripts, I'm going to remind them of the incredibly inexpensive training available to help them move to a more stable, effective operating system.

Consultant Example

Let's say that your prospect is experiencing a morale problem. You happen to be one of the foremost experts in the area. Here's what you know from your experience:

- Management rarely knows the source of a morale problem.
- Even when their employees tell them precisely what the reason is, managers tend to discount what they're being told.
- Management has tried a number of approaches, including financial incentives, none of which have worked.
- Most of management's approaches stem from managers' beliefs that employees need "fixing."

Based on this information, how would you answer the six bundling questions that follow? Please indicate your thoughts in the space provided.

1. What are some of the challenges these buyers face?

2. Can bundling help them overcome these challenges?

3. What could I bundle together to make life easier for my customers?

4. What benefits would they gain from these bundles?

5. What benefits would I gain from these bundles?

6. What script(s) would I use to communicate these benefits to my customers?

Just a reminder that our goal is to help you train your mind to bundle offerings. The purpose in offering so many diverse examples is to help you see the vast array of possibilities. Once you get the hang of it, it won't matter what industry you're in; you'll be able to help your company generate more sales *and* profits through bundling.

Here's an approach I might use in our consultant example:

1. What are some of the challenges these buyers face?
   - They have a morale problem that they don't know how to fix.
   - Their team's productivity is a direct reflection of their leadership capabilities.
   - Their career advancement and future compensation depend on their ability to get the team back on track.
   - A temporary fix isn't good enough; if these managers aren't able to prevent future morale issues their careers will almost certainly take a hit.
   - If, through no fault of their own, these managers face limited career advancement possibilities where they are, the likelihood of finding something better at another company is hampered by the existence of a morale problem within their ranks.

2. Can bundling help them overcome these challenges?
   These managers need:
   - Help identifying the source of the morale problem.
   - A methodology for removing the source of the problem.

- An approach for avoiding future morale problems.
- A return to, or better yet, an improvement upon the productivity that existed prior to the morale problem.

Looks like the makings of a bundle to me.

3. What could I bundle together to make life easier for my customers?

- One bundle might include simply assessing employee morale, identifying the source of the morale problem, and providing a solution.
- A second bundle might include all of the above *plus* some facilitated meetings in which the wounds of the morale experience have a chance to heal under my guidance.
- A third bundle might include the assessment, identification, and elimination of the morale problem, as well as facilitated meetings *and* managerial training that would offer managers some insights into the types of issues that create morale problems and how to avoid them.
- A fourth bundle might include the previous three *plus* one or two coaching sessions for the managers and some employee interviews to assess the manager's progress with his or her new skills.
- A fifth bundle might extend the coaching and follow up employee interviews over several months.

4. What benefits would they gain from these bundles?

- All of the bundles will eliminate the pain that the managers and employees are experiencing and return productivity to previous levels.
- The second bundle would speed healing and increase the likelihood that productivity would increase beyond prior levels.
- The third bundle would add the element of prevention for the manager. It doesn't bode well for managers' careers or compensation when they experience a series of morale problems.
- The fourth bundle recognizes the fact that training has limited impact. Anyone who has attended any type of seminar or workshop, then tried to implement what they've learned, inevitably wishes that they'd asked more questions during the program. Coaching sessions would fill this learning gap.
- The fifth bundle recognizes that we, as human beings, are

creatures of habit—that we often, especially in times of stress, revert to old habits. Increasing the number of coaching sessions would increase the likelihood that the managers will develop new habits to replace the old ones.

5. What benefits would I gain from these bundles?

- With each bundle I gain increased revenues and higher profits. The value of my bundle is directly related to the value the customer gains.
- With the first bundle, managers get a solution to a problem, but the solution will probably be short lived. Why? Because managers are creatures of habit. The odds are that they'll make the same mistake several times before learning their lesson. This means that morale, at best, could be a rollercoaster ride as the manager goes through cycles of making the mistake, recovering, making the mistake, and recovering again. If the manager fails to learn the lesson, his or her career will likely falter.
- The second bundle increases value by healing the rift between manager and employees. A good working relationship promotes greater productivity. We tend to do our best to help people we really like. That's why productivity can rise above previous levels. Increased productivity equals increased value.
- The third bundle *dramatically* improves value because it adds the element of prevention. Managers who avoid morale problems don't experience the lost productivity and the hits it puts on their careers and compensation.
- The fourth bundle offers more value yet, but the value increase isn't as dramatic as is experienced in moving from bundle two to bundle three. While it's true that more of the training sticks with one or two coaching sessions, the result is only marginally better than without coaching.
- The fifth bundle offers the greatest value because it involves changing habits. Once something we do or say becomes a habit, that becomes our fall back position. Bill Russell, the basketball hall-of-fame Boston Celtic center who was renowned for his shot-blocking ability, watched tapes of other players to look for the things that created stress for them and how they

reacted under stress. In the game, he used that knowledge to create stress so that he could anticipate their shots and block them.

When you develop new habits—not new skills, but the habit of employing these skills—you'll return to that skill whenever you're under stress. If you want a sense for how valuable that is, all you have to do is look at what Bill Russell made during his career versus what other players made.

6. What script(s) would I use to communicate these benefits to my customers?

   - For simple problem resolution, I'd talk about eliminating the pain and being able to move forward again.
   - To promote facilitated meetings, I'd ask customers to recall a time when they were unhappy with another person and how long it took them to get over it. I'd point out how much easier it is for an outsider to see common ground and shine a light on it for the benefit of all parties—managers and employees.
   - When suggesting training, I'd stress the fact that the problem he or she is facing is only one of the traps to which managers fall victim, and emphasize that I could help him or her avoid those traps in the future.
   - I'd explain that one or two coaching sessions provide them with the opportunity to ask the follow up questions that inevitably surface during implementation. The follow-up interviews with employees not only give the manager a sense for how well the healing is going, but allows you as facilitator to plant seeds that highlight the manager's efforts in creating an enjoyable work environment.
   - To establish the value of the extended coaching sessions, I'd use the Bill Russell example to show the value of developing new habits.

If I may, I'd like to add one more example. I have not offered an example from an industry or profession that's highly regulated. Let's look at investment advisory services to see whether there are opportunities to bundle offerings when there are severe limitations on what can be included in marketing messages/materials. You know the drill. Put yourself in the shoes of someone who helps people establish their personal financial goals—that first home, kids' college, retirement, their legacy—and then fill in the blanks.

Investment Advisory Example

It's time to change hats again. You're an investment adviser who has all the same tools as your competitors—insurance programs, stocks, bonds, mutual funds, professional money managers. Your customers' goals are also very similar—home ownership, college education for their kids, a comfortable retirement, and a financial legacy. Your challenge is to distinguish yourself from your competitors. Bundling seems to offer some promise but, in order to use it effectively, you need to be able to answer the following questions.

1. What are some of the challenges these buyers face?

2. Can bundling help them overcome these challenges?

3. What could I bundle together to make life easier for my customers?

4. What benefits would they gain from these bundles?

5. What benefits would I gain from these bundles?

6. What script(s) would I use to communicate these benefits to my customer?

Ready? By the way, if the list of challenges didn't dissuade you from wanting to be an investment adviser, consider yourself stout of heart. If I were that brave, here's what I would expect to see and do.

1. What are some of the challenges these buyers face?

   - They don't like to face their mortality.
   - They don't have much, if any, background in how to evaluate various insurance and investment products, so they're left trusting someone else to advice them—not a very comfortable position for any of us to be in.
   - There are a lot more fun things to do.
   - They haven't done a very good job of keeping their financial records so locating those records will be time consuming. Oh, did I mention that it isn't much fun?
   - They despise all the paperwork involved.
   - They're embarrassed to admit how little wealth they've accumulated over the years or how many mistakes they've made previously. Who among us enjoys appearing stupid?
   - Dreams fade in the face of daily living.

2. Can bundling help them overcome these challenges?

   - You can bundle fun into the program.
   - You can add lifestyle tips to the program.
   - You can take some of the paperwork burden off them by filling in the necessary forms so that all they have to do is sign.
   - You can add pertinent information for stage of their life.

3. What could I bundle together to make life easier for my customers?

   - There are a number of things in the list that aren't a lot of fun —facing our mortality, getting records together, doing paperwork, admitting our mistakes. One of the things you can do is create a game that visually tracks their progress toward their goal. You could use pictures of that bass boat, the home at the lake, their kids dressed in caps and gowns in front of Harvard law, medical, or business school. Or how about location pictures from their dream vacation or, better yet, creating a computer screen saver so that they can see their dream every day, along with a graphic showing how close they are? Don't forget to award points for doing the paperwork.

- You could bundle in monthly, quarterly, or semiannual review meetings based on their preferences to keep the dream alive, as well as reevaluating their ever-changing lifestyles.
- You could provide cost saving tips, travel tips, and healthcare tips all designed to enhance their lifestyles. That is what you're selling, isn't it?
- As your clients' kids get closer to college age, you could provide independent reviews of various colleges based on their kids' interests. Rather than inundating them with a ton of information all at once, trickle in information about the various grant, loan, and funding programs available for kids' education. Share with them the various approaches parents have used in dealing with college costs—everything from "we can help out from time to time, but we can't fund your education" to reimbursing them for achieving certain grade point averages to paying the full tab for them
- When retirement is just around the corner, again, you could use the trickle approach. Send them information on Medicare coverage, long-term care coverage, what their social security benefits are expected to be, or what level of withdrawal they'll need to make from their retirement plans for the lifestyle they envision.
- The key in all of this bundling is to inform them in advance of what to expect so that their natural fears and reluctance abate as their confidence in you rises.

4. What benefits would they gain from these bundles?

- Time savings, because you're taking over the paperwork
- More time savings, because they're not having to spend time

trying to track you down to be able to respond to questions with which they have little, if any, familiarity

- Fun, in the form of games or contests, designed to help them get through the initial stages of information gathering quickly
- Greater understanding of finance, insurance, and the various approaches available to them, because you're using the trickle method to educate rather than the fire hose approach. You're also only providing what's relevant to their particular stage of life, which heightens their interest in the material.
- You're providing periodic reviews, according to their level of interest, which shows that you respect their wishes, care about their welfare. These reviews also recognize that unexpected occurs more frequently than we'd like to admit, and these occurrences often require changes to the plan. Finally, your ability to help them deal with these surprises, pleasant or unpleasant as they might be, indicate that you have alternatives for any contingency
- These periodic reviews, when combined with the game format/metrics, help the buyers stay focused on their long-term goals and avoid the costly distractions that could prevent them from achieving those goals.

5. What benefits would I gain from these bundles?

- Your client retention rate will be much higher. People enjoy working with those who can make tedious tasks fun. They also appreciate advisers who help them stay focused.
- You can charge additional fees based on the level of service the buyer desires. Quarterly visits are more valuable than annual visits. I hope you noticed that I didn't say that quarterly visits are more *costly* than annual visits. The cost you incur is not your customers' concern. Customers are only concerned with the value they receive. Don't allow the fact that something costs you more to drive your prices higher. Make sure that the value rises faster than your cost.
- Using the trickle education system, you end up with better educated buyers who make decisions and take action more quickly, thereby saving you time and energy.

- Your ability to help you clients stay focused means that they're likely to build their asset base more quickly than others will. The larger their portfolio grows, the greater their need for financial advice, the greater their need for your services. Your fees/commissions rise as their wealth grows
- You're more likely to get referrals because of the high satisfaction/loyalty rate you experience with your clients

6. What script(s) would I use to communicate these benefits to my customers?

   - We think that planning your future should be fun. We've devised a game that helps you see your dream becoming a reality. It'll show you what's worked for you and what needs changing so that your dream becomes a reality. The game could combine smaller short-term goals—that dream trip with the longer term retirement and legacy goals.
   - We don't think you should have to complete lengthy forms with questions that don't make sense to you. That's why we've taken over the preparation of the documents for you. We'll base the answers on what you've told us that you want to achieve and the risk that you're comfortable with, then review them with you so that you have a thorough understanding before signing. We'll take as much time as needed for you to get comfortable with the responses before signing.
   - One of the things we've experienced is that day-to-day living often distracts people from their long-term goals. We experience that ourselves. That's why we use advisers to help us stay focused on our long-term goals. We provide that service for you through periodic visits. The frequency of those visits depend upon your personal preference and the rate of change occurring in your life.
   - As you're living your dreams and thinking about your legacy, we visit with the people who are going to benefit from that legacy to help them understand your wishes and the approaches you want utilized in achieving that legacy. It's sad, but all too often people's plan for enhancing the lives of others doesn't quite hit the mark because those charged with implementing the plan didn't know what was intended.

As you can see, the limitations to bundling that we might envision, be they regulatory, buyer price sensitivity, or competitors' offerings, really only exist in our own minds. As you gain more experience in bundling your offerings, of adding icing to both your and your customers' cakes, you'll enjoy greater revenues and profits. The key questions to ask, then, in establishing an effective bundle are:

1. What are some of the challenges these buyers face?
2. Can bundling help them overcome these challenges?
3. What could I bundle together to make life easier for my customers?
4. What benefits would they gain from these bundles?
5. What benefits would I gain from these bundles?
6. What script(s) would I use to communicate these benefits to my customers?

Now that you know how to bundle offerings, let's find out how to get them to buy those offerings. That's the goal of Chapter 6.

Executive Summary

1. Bundling helps you:
   - Sweeten the deal for your customers
   - Increase your average ticket price
   - Increase your employees' productivity
   - Reduce your risks

2. Bundles target the same value propositions we've discussed in earlier chapters:
   - Image
   - Innovation
   - Time savings

3. When bundling, we take the three value propositions listed in number two above and explode back out to the nine value attributes:
   - Speed
   - Friendliness
   - Integrity
   - Dependability

- Convenience
- Image
- Service

- Innovation
- Knowledgeable sales people

Using these nine valuable attributes in our sales scripts allows us to help customers see value in our existing offerings that they, and we, often overlook. This helps us avoid continuously adding new features and costs to our offerings.

4. Bundling is available for any offering in any industry or profession.

5. The key questions to ask in establishing an effective bundle are:

- What are some of the challenges these buyers face?
- Can bundling help them overcome these challenges?
- What could I bundle together to make life easier for my customers?
- What benefits would they gain from these bundles?
- What benefits would I gain from these bundles?
- What script(s) would I use to communicate these benefits to my customers?

CHAPTER 6

Avoiding No: Using Options to Close the Sale

I'm sure that some of you are scratching your heads thinking "Wait a minute, Dale! You told us to walk away from prospects who don't value what we offer. Now you're suggesting that we avoid "No" so that we can close the sale. What's up?

You're right. In Chapter 4, in the section "Little or No Interest," I said, "If the prospect places little or no value on what you offer, walk away." I made the same suggestion with regard to those prospects who demonstrate "some interest" in your offerings. I'm not changing my mind; in these situations you want the prospect to say "No!"

In this chapter I'm referring to a different situation—one in which you've already identified the prospect as being one who values what you're offering and is willing to pay a premium to get it. Our goal is to help you avoid losing these prospects to your competitors. How? By offering options that make it easy for your prospects to say "Yes."

Options allow you to offer your prospects different mixes of the essential elements they value. Well-constructed options also offer your prospects various budget alternatives from which to choose. Enough of the 30,000 foot view; the keys to effective use of options are:

1. Offering options. As obvious as this seems, some businesspeople don't offer options.
2. Clearly delineating the options and the value each provides.
3. Pricing each option to assure higher levels of customer satisfaction.
4. Deciding whether to sell up or sell down; that is, do you start with the low price option or the high price option?

Let's look at each of these to see what's involved and how each helps you close the sale.

Offering Options

I can't begin to tell you how often over my twenty years as a consultant I've seen business owners offer one option with one price point. This is particularly true in the service sector, where bankers, financial advisers, consultants, and other professionals offer only one solution to their prospects' problems.

Place yourself in the role of the prospect. If you're offered only one solution with one price point, what are your choices? Yes or no, right? Now imagine that an enlightened banker or financial adviser created three bundles using the techniques we discussed in Chapter 5. What choices do you have now? Three different options, each designed for a different budget and a different set of needs. What are the odds that none of these bundles is going to fit your needs? Pretty low, aren't they? Why?

Education

One reason that at least one of these options is going to work for the banker or financial adviser is that they helped you think through what you're really trying to accomplish. You're not interested in borrowing money; you're interested in buying new equipment, funding a seasonal cash flow shortfall, or taking advantage of a new opportunity. Similarly, you don't want to own investments or insurance policies; you want the wealth building and protection advantages they afford.

With options, these lenders and advisers are helping you gain a clear understanding of what it is that you're trying to accomplish and why it's important to you. In essence, by helping you make conscious choices, they are educating you as to what's important to you and why.

Budget Considerations

In addition, they're helping you determine what is affordable for you by offering you options designed for different budgets. Having several different monthly payment options helps you determine which loan is most affordable. Similarly, knowing what the prices are for various insurance programs and investment options helps you decide which program is right for you.

As you can see, the odds of you buying go up dramatically when you have options from which to choose. The education you received and the budget considerations from which you can choose make it easy for you to say "Yes."

Now that we understand the importance of the first key to using options effectively, offering options, let's turn to the second key, clearly stating the advantages and disadvantages of each option, and see what doors it opens for us.

Delineating Options

Explaining options is often easier to do with products than with services. It's easy for a customer to understand the difference between a McDonald's sandwich, meal, and supersize meal. Remembering which level of service you bought from a financial adviser, what it included, and what you're going to gain from that offering is another story. Whether you're being offered products or services, it's important that you, as a consumer, know the advantages and disadvantages of each option.

To help you get a feel for what delineating options involves, let's revisit the consultant example we used in Chapter 5. The client in this example had a morale problem. During the exercise, we identified five different bundles, or options, that could be offered to this client to help resolve this problem. Those bundles were:

1. Assessing employee morale, identifying the source of the morale problem, and providing a solution to that problem.
2. All of bundle one *plus* some facilitated meetings in which the wounds of the morale experience have a chance to heal under your guidance.
3. Assessment, identification, and elimination of the morale problem, facilitated meetings (in essence, bundles one and two), *and* managerial training which offer managers insights into the types of issues that create morale problems and how to avoid them.

4. All of bundle three *plus* one or two coaching sessions for the managers as well as some employee interviews to assess the manager's progress with his or her new skills.

5. The extension of coaching and follow-up employee interviews in bundle four over several months while holding the other aspects of that bundle constant.

Before we go any further, I'm going to ask you to change hats again. To this point in this chapter, I've asked you to consider situations from the buyer's perspective. For this exercise, I want you to don the seller's hat. You're the consultant in this example. You've identified five potential bundles above for your prospect. Where do you go from here?

Some of the bundles only indicate what you're going to do. Others also give some hint as to why you're adding that feature to the bundle. Generally, though, there isn't a clear indication of what the advantages and disadvantages of each option are. Let's see if we can clean this up a bit.

The first thing we want to do is limit the number of options. Typically, more than three options make the choice more difficult for the buyer. To illustrate this point, I'd like you to recall your visit to a restaurant with lots of variations on the same meal. Let's say that you're hungry for a burger and you enter a new restaurant that specializes in them. A quick glance at the menu shows that they have close to a dozen different types of burgers. In a situation like this, have you ever found yourself asking, "Can I just get a cheeseburger with fries?"

Our minds resist complexity. The more complex the decision (a dozen burger choices), the more likely we are to go with the simplest, least expensive option available. If, however, we narrow the choices (burger with standard toppings, a cheeseburger with standard toppings) and include additional alternatives (the ability to add a salad or fries to either), we've simplified the choices enough that the buyer will consider adding those alternatives.

Returning to our consultant example, which of the five bundles would you choose in creating options for your prospect? In the space provided below each option, list your reasons for including or rejecting this item from the list of options you offer.

1. Assessing employee morale, identifying the source of the morale problem, and providing a solution to that problem.

2. All of bundle one *plus* some facilitated meetings in which the wounds of the morale experience have a chance to heal under your guidance.

3. Assessment, identification, and elimination of the morale problem, facilitated meetings (in essence, bundles one and two), *and* managerial training which offer managers insights into the types of issues that create morale problems and how to avoid them.

4. All of bundle three *plus* one or two coaching sessions for the managers as well as some employee interviews to assess the manager's progress with his or her new skills.

5. The extension of coaching and follow-up employee interviews in bundle four over several months while holding the other aspects of that bundle constant.

Once again, I've provided my analysis for your consideration below. There is nothing that says that my thoughts are any better than yours. My answers simply provide another perspective on the issues and another approach to evaluating available options.

1. Assessing employee morale, identifying the source of the morale problem, and providing a solution to that problem:

Options one and two have similar value. The addition of the facilitated meetings doesn't require a significant time investment for either your prospect or you. Often, one meeting will accomplish this goal. If the problem is so severe that it can't be accomplished in a meeting or two, then neither option one nor two might be viable for this prospect. For the purpose of this example, let's assume that this isn't an especially severe problem and that facilitating one or two meetings isn't going to add much to the value or price of the offering. Based on that assumption, I'd choose option two over option one.

2. All of bundle one *plus* some facilitated meetings in which the wounds of the morale experience have a chance to heal under your guidance:

   For all of the reasons mentioned in number one above, I'd choose option two as one of the options I'd offer.

3. Assessment, identification, and elimination of the morale problem, facilitated meetings (in essence, bundles one and two), *and* managerial training which offer managers insights into the types of issues that create morale problems and how to avoid them:

   Option three adds a preventative aspect to option two that has tremendous value. If managers keeping making the same mistakes over and over again or keep stumbling along the path in developing their managerial skills, poor morale with its attendant costs will become a regular occurrence in this organization. Training alone, though, often leaves managers on their own in implementing what they learned. It's one of the major reasons why training alone has such a poor return on investment. That's why I think option four has greater value than option three.

4. All of bundle three *plus* one or two coaching sessions for the managers, as well as some employee interviews to assess the manager's progress with his or her new skills:

   Option four will be my second choice for the reasons cited in option three above. Managers who have been trained in new skills inevitably need guidance in applying what they've learned. They also need feedback from their direct reports to affirm or refute their perceptions of how well they're doing. So option four is my second choice.

5. The extension of coaching and follow-up employee interviews in bundle four for several months while holding the other aspects of that bundle constant.

Option five is the best alternative for long-term results. It affords managers the opportunity to accelerate their learning and develop new habits that will benefit them, their employees, and the company. Option five is one of the choices I'd offer.

Now that we've narrowed the number of options from five to three, a more manageable number for buyers, we want to become clear about the advantages and disadvantages of each of these remaining options. I've purposely kept price out of the mix in this example for several reasons. First, I'd like you to gain experience in delineating offerings on the basis of the results your prospect will get, not on price. Second, later in this chapter I'm going to show you how to use price to guide buyers' decisions. Third, I don't want to add complexity to the exercise by mixing the two concepts, delineation and price, at this time.

The three remaining options are listed below. In the space provided below each, indicate what you believe the prospect gains *and* foregoes with each option. It's important that you state both to assure that the prospect understands that you're a person of integrity, that you want them to make an informed decision and that you care enough to make sure they get what they want. For each of the following options, what does the prospect gain and forego?

1. Assessment, identification, and elimination of morale problem *plus* up to two facilitated meetings in which the wounds of the morale experience have a chance to heal under your guidance.

2. Assessment, identification, and elimination of the morale problem, up to two facilitated meetings to heal morale, one managerial training class, two coaching sessions for each of the managers, and two follow-up employee interviews with randomly

selected employees to assess the manager's progress with his or her new skills.

3. Assessment, identification, and elimination of the morale problem, up to two facilitated meetings to heal morale, one managerial training class, two coaching sessions per month for each of the managers for four months, and four follow up employee interviews with randomly selected employees to assess the manager's progress with his or her new skills.

Let's compare notes. Here are the advantages and disadvantages I see:

1. Assessment, identification, and elimination of morale problem *plus* up to two facilitated meetings in which the wounds of the morale experience have a chance to heal under your guidance:

    This option removes the pain and frustration you and your employees are experiencing. It also creates a nurturing, encouraging environment that allows your employees to return to or exceed previous levels of productivity. This option does not, however, assure that the problem won't resurface or that other issues affecting morale won't appear. Since we, as human beings, are creatures of habit, it's likely that, in times of stress, you and your managers will revert to old habits and that morale will, once again, deteriorate.

2. Assessment, identification, and elimination of the morale problem, up to two facilitated meetings to heal morale, one managerial training class, two coaching sessions for each of the managers, and two follow-up employee interviews with randomly selected employees to assess the manager's progress with his or her new skills:

    Option two provides the problem resolution advantages of option one *plus* it increases the likelihood that morale and productivity will remain high. Why? Because the training is designed to highlight the leading causes of morale problems and the methodologies you and your managers can use to avoid them.

The two coaching sessions are designed to help you and your managers implement effectively what you learned during training. These sessions afford opportunities to have implementation questions and challenges addressed. These sessions have the additional advantage of accelerating learning and the achievement of a positive, encouraging, and enjoyable work environment.

Finally, feedback is an essential element in any endeavor, which is why we've built two sets of employee interviews into this option. Employees will be interviewed twice after the training is completed. The first set of interviews will occur three weeks after the training; the second, three weeks after that. Employee feedback from these interviews will provide you and your managers with input on how well the implementation is going and whether or not any of the managers are sliding back to old habits. As you can see, option two is designed to help you achieve longer term results.

The one thing that option two does not provide is the development of new habits. Two coaching sessions, typically, are not enough to help you and your managers develop new habits. What you'll discover is that when your managers become stressed, and they will, they'll return to old habits—the ones they employed prior to the training which opens the door to another round of morale issues. Option three is designed to deal with this challenge.

3. Assessment, identification, and elimination of the morale problem, up to two facilitated meetings to heal morale, one managerial training class, two coaching sessions per month for each of the managers for four months, and four follow-up employee interviews with randomly selected employees to assess the manager's progress with his or her new skills:

Option three provides all of the benefits of the options one and two *plus* it helps you and your managers develop new habits. Just as Bill Russell, the basketball hall-of-fame center for the

Boston Celtics, developed new habits by employing what he learned from watching tapes of his competitors, your managers, through additional coaching and employee interviews, will be able to develop the habit of employing what they learned.

All of us revert to old behaviors, our habits, when we're under stress. The advantage that option three affords is the ability to develop new, more productive managerial habits that become the safe place you and your managers go when under stress. These new habits increase the likelihood that you and your team will gain the greatest long-term benefits from your efforts.

Pricing the Options

The goal in pricing options is to help buyers choose the option that's in *their* best interest. You'll notice that I didn't say the one that generates the greatest revenue for you, although they are often the same. There are several reasons why I'm suggesting this approach:

1. It's ethical and, despite all the unethical behavior we hear about in the news, ethical approaches to doing business promote long-term relationships with customers. Long-term relationships provide consistent revenues and profits that business owners relish.
2. Each of us is born with a sixth sense that lets us know very quickly when someone's actions are self-serving. If your prospects get the sense that you care more about your revenues than them, you're not only likely to lose this sale, but all future sales to these buyers.
3. Everyone has budget constraints. Respecting the fact that prospects' budgets may not permit them to choose the best option available leaves the door open for them to get the rest of what they need at a future date.

These are the reasons why your pricing should direct prospects to the option that best suits their needs. Let's return to our consulting example.

Consulting Example: Value Calculation

We'll use some hypothetical numbers to help us calculate the value and price of each of the three options identified above. First we determine what value the prospect will get from eliminating the morale problem. There are a number of benefits for us to consider:

- The frustration that both employees and managers experience ends.
- Employee absenteeism, a common symptom of a morale problem, ends and employees return to normal productivity.
- Attracting good employees is easier when there is a healthy, enjoyable work environment.
- Employee turnover drops along with its attendant costs.

Frustration

What's the value of reducing frustration? It's a well-established fact that stress creates health problems. Frustration is a byproduct of stress. If the stress continues for months or years, it's going to take a toll on both the manager's and employees' health. Some of you are probably thinking that unhappy employees eventually leave. That has not been my experience. Often the fear of the unknown, the financial commitments employees make in the form of house and car payments, and the volatility of the job market keep many people in jobs they hate.

How costly can this frustration be? Let's say that health-care costs are rising, on average, 12 percent a year. This group is experiencing 25 percent more health issues than the average; therefore, their premiums are likely to be 25 percent higher—15 percent a year, 3 percent more than the average. If their health-care coverage currently costs $20,000 a year, their premiums are going rise an additional $600 ($20,000 × 3%) the first year and more rapidly in the future because all future increases will be calculated on this higher base premium.

Absenteeism

The cost of absenteeism typically shows up in two ways—overtime and temporary help. The work's got to get done, right? Whether people are showing up to work or not, customers expect to be served well. Let's assume that this prospect is spending $85,000 a year on overtime and another $40,000 a year on temporary help. You've already discussed these costs with him and he has agreed that if employees showed up for work and worked at their current capability, there would be no need for overtime or temporary help. So there's $125,000 of potential savings in year one—a savings that could be annuitized if the company maintains a healthy, happy work environment. For those of you who may not be familiar with the term "annuitized," it simply means year in, year out. In other words, this prospect could save a minimum of $125,000 per year in overtime and temporary help costs for many years in the future by maintaining a healthy, happy work environment.

Attracting Good Employees
When prospects are able to attract talented people, their hiring costs go down because people are seeking employment with their company instead of their company having to pursue candidates. Also, the learning curve for talented people is shorter than for the average worker. This shorter learning curve translates into less lost productivity.

Further, talented people are more likely to see opportunities to improve the way a business operates, which can increase productivity even further. We'll assume that for this prospect, attracting talented people would add an additional $30,000 a year to their bottom line due to lower hiring costs and increased productivity. Please don't get too caught up in the reasonableness of these hypothetical numbers. The numbers are for illustration, not accuracy.

Employee Turnover Drops
Some of the potential cost savings are already included in the "Attracting Good Employees" segment above. If, however, employee turnover drops and this prospect doesn't have to find as many new employees, savings grow even more. The fact that employees are reluctant to change jobs on their own doesn't mean that you won't have turnover. When employees' performance is poor for extended periods of time you'll end up making the choice for them. One way or another, turnover will exist. Let's say that there's an additional $50,000 of savings available on top of the $30,000 identified above.

Let's tally the results:

Frustration	$ 600
Absenteeism	$125,000
Attracting good employees	$ 30,000
Employee turnover drops	$ 50,000
Total financial benefit available	$205,600

Now that we have some numbers with which to work, let's calculate the value of each option for the prospect.

Option one essentially eliminates the pain the prospect is currently experiencing. The pain lies in the frustration and the absenteeism. There is, undoubtedly, psychic value to eliminating the pain that goes well beyond the $600 potential health-care savings listed above, but let's stay with the numbers we have to keep the example simple. Option one has a combined value of $125,600, the value of frustration and absenteeism, in the first year. Remember, any of these options will be annuitized—will provide annual savings—if the prospect avoids repeating the mistakes that caused the morale problem in the first place.

Option two also eliminates the pain, but it also has the potential to significantly lower employee turnover which adds another $50,000 of value, bringing the value of option two to $175,600 for the first year. Again, this savings can be annuitized.

Option three adds the benefit of attracting good employees. Typically it takes years for companies to gain reputations for being employers of choice—companies for whom people want to work. I'm including the "attracting good employees" benefit in option three because this long-term benefit isn't likely to be gained without the extensive coaching and feedback option three affords. Since option three encompasses all of the benefits listed above, its value in the first year is $205,600.

Let's recap the financial value of each option:

Option one	$125,600
Option two	$175,600
Option three	$205,600

Given these values it's relatively easy to calculate the price of each option.

Consulting Example: Price Calculation

Your business philosophy—remember, you're the seller in this situation —is that you want to provide your prospects with a minimum of a 100 percent return the first year. That means that the price of each of the above options is one half of the option's value. Here are the price points this calculation would create:

Option one $ 62,800 ($125,600 ×50%)
Option two $ 87,800 ($175,600 ×50%)
Option three $102,800 ($205,600 ×50%)

Remember that our goal is to guide this prospect to the greatest benefit he or she can get. That benefit lies in option three because it involves the development of new habits. As good fortune would have it, in this example there isn't a great deal of price difference between options two or three, especially when you consider the likelihood that the savings will be annuitized is greater with option three. The additional $25,000 cost of option three over option two pales in comparison to a second year of $205,600 savings.

What if the price gap between two and three wasn't so narrow? What if option three's price is $125,600 versus the $87,600 of option two? With a gap that large, it may be more difficult for prospects to choose option three. What do you do then? Remember, your goal is to help buyers choose the best option available to them, and you know that option three offers the greatest long-term benefit.

The answer is "narrow the gap." You can do that in one of two ways—you can either reduce the price of option three or raise the price of option two. I'm sure some of you are recalling my comment above about the value of ethical business practices and wondering "Is raising the price of option two ethical when the value didn't change?" I believe it is. You may or may not agree with me, after all ethics is a lot more subjective and more difficult to define than many of us would like to think. Having acknowledged the legitimacy of your concern, here are my reasons for raising the price of option two.

Option two has a much greater chance of producing *long-term results* than option one, which means that the likelihood of annuitizing savings is significantly higher—not as high as option three, but significantly higher than with option one. In essence, the probability that the prospect will enjoy a second year's savings is much higher with option two than option one. That's why I wouldn't have an ethical dilemma in raising the price of option two to narrow the gap between options two and three.

Again, my goal is to help prospects get the best return on their investment. The fact that my revenues will rise as well doesn't alter the fact that the prospect will get the best long-term results from option three. Indeed, it's often true that when your prospects make decisions that are in their best interests, those decisions will benefit you as well. The key is to make their interests your top priority.

Enough on ethics, let's get back to our example. There is a wider gap in prices between options one and two. In my opinion, that should be the case. Option one has a much lower potential for producing long-term results. I would not narrow the gap in this instance. Instead, I would use the price differential between one and two to help the prospect understand the small probability of a long-term solution coming from option one. Now that we have an approach for pricing each option, the question becomes "Do we sell up or down?"

Deciding to Sell Up or Down

Should you start high and lower your price as car dealers do? Or is it better to start with the base offering and work your way up? Once again I'm going to refer you to that sage, Robert Cialdini, and his book, *Influence: Science and Practice.*[11] Professor Cialdini cites studies he's done that show it's better to sell down. His rationale is that it's more difficult for a person to say "No" to a second request when it's a smaller request.

If that isn't substantive enough evidence for you, let's take a look at an infomercial with which I'm sure that you're all familiar—the infamous knives. I'm going to paraphrase the sales script since I can't recall the name of the knives, the actual script, or the prices. The following script does, however, illustrate the concept of selling down.

You're watching television and an ad comes on for these amazing knives that cut through nails and still remain razor sharp. The demonstration is impressive. You're anxiously awaiting the price. $59.95! Hmm, that's a little steep. But wait a minute, they're offering a special deal. If you call right now, you'll save $20. Well, $39.95 is a lot more reasonable, but wait! They're adding some more knives if you're the one of the first one hundred to call. On and on and on until three offers later you can get the whole package for $19.95, but you've got to call now!

Did you, at some point, begin to question the quality of the knives? Did your skepticism keep you from reaching for the phone with your credit card in hand? Or did you think, "What have I got to lose? It's only $20." Obviously there are plenty of people in the latter category because these folks keep running the infomercials despite the fact that television time is very expensive.

This is the classic example of selling down. You may not like it. It may sound cheesy to you. It may conjure up nightmarish images of plaid-jacketed, used-car salesmen, but it works. Here's the good news. You can sell down without having people think that you're cheesy or a reincarnated used-car salesman. In this and future examples, I'm going to demonstrate that it is possible to sell down and retain your dignity.

Let's see how we can use the sell-down technique in this consultant example. We begin by looking at the pricing of our three options again:

Option one	$ 62,800
Option two	$ 87,800
Option three	$102,800

The sell-down technique says that we start with the highest price option and work our way down the price scale. That means in the proposal we create for this prospect the $102,800 option appears first, the $87,800 option second and the $62,800 option third. Now that we have the proper presentation sequence, let's see what language we might use to retain our dignity while presenting these options. Here's one presentation approach we could use:

"I'm sure that you want to maximize the return on your investment, so the first option I'm proposing is one that provides not only a solution to your immediate morale problem, but the ability to prevent future recurrences with their associated costs." I'd go through each of the benefits the high-end bundle affords, then shut up and give your prospects a chance to respond. You'll find out quickly if this option exceeds their budget.

If option one is too large for their budget, you drop down to option two, but emphasize what they're giving up by dropping down a notch. If that's still too large, you move down to your lowest price option. Again, you emphasize what they're giving up and how much the odds of gaining long-term results goes down with this option.

Let's say that the lowest price option is the one they choose. You'll still have the peace of mind that comes with knowing that you've done everything in your power to help them make an informed decision. Having said that, I'd highly recommend you include the advantages and disadvantages of each option in your written proposal (the one they sign) to protect yourself against claims that you didn't make them aware of the risks they were taking with the low-price option.

There is one more possible outcome; the prospect may say that even your lowest price option is too high. What do you do? Go back to my advice in Chapter 4 and walk away. This buyer isn't suffering sufficiently to want to make a change, and there isn't anything you can do about that.

I'm sure that those of you in product sales, especially retail sales, are thinking "I don't do proposals. Even if I did, my customers aren't going to do that much reading. I've got to get my message across quickly." Indeed you do. Let's see how we might use the lessons learned from the consultant example above.

Retail Product Sales: Home Theater Systems

Let's say that you're selling home theater systems. Using what you've just learned, you've decided to offer three options—a high-end system, a mid-range system, and a low-end system. To make this example a little more useful, let's capture the pricing information from Chapter 3 in Table 6-1.

Table 6-1. Home Theater System Prices

Home Theater Systems	Bose	Samsung 5.1 channel system	Sony's Bravia 5.1 channel system
Entry level	$1,000	$400	$200
Top of the line	$3,800	$900	$700

We're going to assume that you've chosen the Bose top-of-the-line system as your high-end system, Samsung's top-of-the-line model as your mid-range system, and Sony's entry-level system as your low price option. How are you going to succinctly delineate these offerings? Remember you only have a few lines on a product card to guide your prospect. Make your pitch in the space provided below each option:

Bose top-of-the-line system

Samsung top-of-the-line system

Sony entry-level system

Here's what I came up with:

Bose system	For those who want the ultimate experience in sight and sound and those who want only the best: $3,800
Samsung system	For discerning listeners and viewers looking for high quality at an affordable price: $900
Sony system	For occasional users and people with limited budgets who demand quality and dependability: $200

As you can see, I took the liberty of including the price of each since they were already identified in Table 6-1. Why? I wanted to help the customer identify what's important to them as well as what's affordable for them. Until they see these product summaries, your prospects are likely to avoid your salespeople. Why? Because they didn't know what options were available or what price ranges existed. Once they have this information, they feel more comfortable approaching a salesperson. Why? They have a frame of reference from which to work. One of the challenges buyers face is the fear of appearing stupid because they don't know what they want or need. Providing even a small amount of information can help them overcome this fear, allowing them to move forward quickly with confidence. Now that we've delineated and priced each of these offerings, let's see whether the options and pricing we've chosen are going to help your prospects make the best decisions for them.

Certainly, these summaries give prospects a quick frame of reference for identifying their interests. People who always want the best know which model fits their needs. The question that remains is, "Is there $3,800 in the budget to get the best?" If not, are they going to lower their expectations and go with the mid-range price or wait until they've had a chance to save up enough to get what they really want?

Prospects who don't feel that they can really tell the difference between the Bose and Samsung systems, or that the difference isn't sufficient to warrant the Bose price premium, are typically going to choose the Samsung option.

Buyers who rent an occasional movie, rarely buy CDs and DVDs, or are just getting started in their jobs are likely to opt for the Sony entry level model. So it seems that we've done a good job of delineating the options for the customer. Have we done a good job on the budget side? Let's see whether another configuration might be more effective.

Typically, you don't want to lower the price of your best option for the same reasons that we didn't in the consultant example—the customer is getting the best result possible. That leaves us with the two lower options. If you want to narrow the gap between the entry-level system and the mid-range system, you could replace the Sony entry-level model with the Samsung entry-level model. The configuration would then be:

Bose high-end system for the ultimate experience	$3,800
Samsung high-end system for the discerning listener	$ 900
Samsung's entry-level system	$ 400

This approach could eliminate the low end of the market for you—those who aren't willing to pay $400 for a system. While you may lose some, if not all, of this market, you're going to increase the productivity of your sales force. Why? They're generating a larger average sale per customer. Plus, it takes as much time, if not more, to deal with a low-price buyer as it does their wealthier, value-oriented counterparts. The reasons that it takes longer to close a sale to a low-budget prospect is that money is in shorter supply, making it more difficult for that person to decide whether this is a sensible way to spend money. Price buyers, on the other hand, gobble up huge amounts of time trying to get a better price even when they've already decided to make the purchase.

Taking Professor Cialdini's advice, we're going to position our offerings so that the first thing the prospect sees in the home theater section is the top-of-the-line Bose system, then the high-end Samsung system, and finally the low-end Sony or Samsung system. It's the equivalent of selling down.

We've employed all four steps involved in using options. We:

1. Identified options	Bose high end, Samsung high end, and Sony entry level or Samsung low end	
2. Delineated options:	Bose—ultimate experience, no budget limitations	
	Samsung—discerning listeners, some budget limitations	
	Sony—occasional user, limited budget	
3. Priced the options:	Bose	$3,800
	Samsung	$ 900
	Sony	$ 200
4. Sold down:	By positioning our offerings with the highest price first, we accomplish the goal of selling down	

Let's get a little more experience with these tools. As you've probably surmised, I'm trying to give you a look at as many types of businesses and industries as I can so that you can see how universal these concepts are and how easily you can adapt them to any situation you face. One business we've only touched upon briefly is banking. Here's a banking example to fill that void.

Business Loans: Increasing the Close Rate

Most commercial banks separate their business lending function from the deposit/cash management function. For this example, we're going to assume that your company, not you personally, is seeking a loan at the bank.

When you talk to a loan officer about getting a loan for your company, there's an implicit expectation that the company will be moving its deposit accounts as well. Typically, when I review a bank's loan proposal for my clients, the proposal includes the:

- Dollar amount requested.
- Term of the loan (months or years).
- Interest rate.
- Amount of the monthly payment.
- Collateral required.
- Owners' personal guarantees.
- Type of security agreement required.

For those of you who may not be familiar with some of these terms, banks usually require the borrower to agree to a lien on some of its assets so that the bank can, in the event of a default, take possession of those assets and sell them to recoup its money. The assets subject to these liens are called "collateral."

In addition, banks often require the owners to sign personal guarantees which state that if the company fails to repay the loan the owners agree to repay the loan on behalf of the company. As you might imagine, this condition isn't very popular with borrowers. Bankers, on the other hand, feel that if the owner or owners don't have enough confidence in their business plan to feel comfortable offering their personal guarantees, perhaps the plan isn't all that good. It's an ongoing debate that we'll not resolve here. Just know that personal guarantees are usually required.

On top of the collateral and personal guarantees, banks usually seek a blanket security agreement which, in essence, gives the bank access to all assets the company owns. In other words, in the event of default, the bank can take possession of any asset the company owns to satisfy the debt. Some security agreements define more narrowly the range of as-

sets available to the bank and, thus, are not considered "blanket" security agreements.

While I've not had much success in helping clients avoid the personal guarantee condition, I've found it rather easy to avoid the blanket
security agreement for companies that are financially sound. Hopefully,
these brief descriptions will help you as we go through this example.

Once again, here's what the bank's proposal normally includes:

- Dollar amount requested.
- Term of the loan (months or years).
- Interest rate.
- Amount of the monthly payment.
- Collateral required.
- Owners' personal guarantees.
- Type of security agreement required.

What's missing? There are no options! It's a take-it-or-leave-it offer. You and I know that it's easier for prospects to say "No" than it is for
them to say "Yes." So why set ourselves up for the "No"? I can't begin to
tell you how many bank loan officers I've met bemoan their closing rates,
yet fail to offer options. Even when I suggest using options to them, they
resist, saying, "It doesn't matter; price is the only thing borrowers care
about. They'll go down the street for a quarter of a point (percent)." They
will if loan officers don't position themselves to "Avoid No." Let's get on
with our example.

Assume that you are a bank loan officer and you're looking at the
list of items in the proposal. What options might you create? Don't let
the lack of specifics about the loan dissuade you; we're simply looking
for alternatives for each proposal item. I'm purposely not including
numbers at this point to avoid clouding the issue. Indicate your options
next to each item on the list below. I've filled in the dollar amount option to illustrate what I'm seeking.

- Dollar amount requested – amount requested, higher amount,
  lower amount

- Term of the loan (months or years)

- Interest rate

- Amount of the monthly payment

- Collateral required

- Owners' personal guarantees

- Type of security agreement required

What did you come up with? There are no right or wrong answers, just varying approaches. Here are some options I've identified. You'll notice that I've fleshed out the explanation of my options to help you understand why I choose those options.

- Dollar amount requested
    If the dollar amount requested is higher than my board is comfortable approving, I might suggest a smaller loan as well as some ideas on how the prospect could achieve its goals with a smaller loan. Conversely, if the prospect is being ultraconservative in its request, I might suggest that the borrowers eliminate stress for themselves by borrowing a little more money. This latter option also has the advantage of helping me increase my revenues.

- Term of the loan (months or years)

  The term of the loan can have a huge impact on the size of the monthly payment the borrower will face. By extending the term of the loan, you can make the payments more affordable from a cash flow standpoint. By shortening the loan term, you help the borrower save interest cost. This is especially helpful for companies that are generating healthy sums of cash. The key here is to make sure that you don't extend the loan term beyond the life of the underlying assets. In other words, don't do what the automobile companies did and offer a sixty-month loan on a car that only lasts thirty-six to forty-eight months. The borrowers who opted for the sixty-month loan often found themselves needing a new vehicle while still paying on the old one.

- Interest rate

  The interest rate typically varies with time (the term of the loan). Generally, lenders want a higher rate for long-term loans than they do for short-term loans. The theory is that interest rates are less predictable the farther out you go. So we can offer alternative interest rates depending on the term of the loan.

  We can also offer lower rates when we get more collateral or charge higher rates when there isn't adequate collateral available. A *caveat* here: there are bank regulations requiring certain levels of collateralization or security in some form. I'm not familiar with those rules, but they have to be factored into your options. For our purposes, we're going to assume that what we're proposing in the remainder of this example meets those regulatory requirements.

- Amount of the monthly payment

  We've already seen in earlier items that we have several approaches for adjusting the monthly payment. We can increase or decrease the term of the loan, we can charge higher or lower interest rates, and we can accept higher or lower levels of collateral. If you can discern from the prospect what the company can afford in a monthly payment from a cash flow standpoint, often it's easier to start with payment options and work backward to the term, interest rate, and collateral.

- Collateral required

    Different assets have different cash conversion rates. Here are some examples. Banks will typically lend up to 80 percent of accounts receivable because it's fairly easy to collect accounts receivable.

    Inventory, on the other hand, has to be sold before the cash can be collected. The process of selling and then collecting the proceeds can take several months. This protracted time frame for converting inventory to cash, combined with other aspects of the inventory, such as its perishability or the fact that it's specialized and, consequently, has a limited market, can lower the collateral value from 80 percent to as little as 50 percent of the cost of the inventory.

    Banks will typically lend up to 80 percent on new equipment, but only 50 percent on used equipment. Given these parameters we, as bankers, have latitude in offering options to our borrowers.

- Owners' personal guarantees

    The fact that getting personal guarantees is almost industry dogma means that this item affords a wonderful opportunity to distinguish your bank from its competitors *in the right situation.* If you have a particularly strong prospect—its business model has been extremely successful for years and the market's outlook for the future is solid or expanding—you could waive the personal guarantees and dramatically increase your odds of the getting the deal. It also affords you, the banker, greater leverage in seeking a blanket security agreement or more collateral. In essence, you're swapping the owners' personal guarantees for assurances that aren't as objectionable to them.

- Type of security agreement required

    As we discussed above, you can forego the blanket security agreement all together or modify the agreement to limit your access to just certain assets over and above the collateral you have when you have a financially sound borrower. You can also swap the blanket security agreement for additional collateral and personal guarantees.

Now that we have a sense for the alternatives available to us, let's decide what packages make the most sense for our prospects. Despite the fact there are seven items included the proposal, there are really only three things that drive a borrowers' decision on a loan:

- Monthly payment.
- Interest cost.
- Security.

Borrowers want to know what their monthly payment is going to be, what the interest rate is, and how much security they're going to have to provide to the bank. The more security they give, whether in the form of collateral, personal guarantees, or security agreements, the less they have to offer for future loan needs. With that in mind, let's create some options. Remember, we want to limit the number of options to three so that we don't overwhelm the prospect.

Previously in this chapter we began the process by identifying options, delineating them, pricing them, and then developing an approach for selling down. That doesn't have to be the sequence. Often it's easier to delineate prospects' needs first, and then develop the options. I believe that's true for this example. In the following pages, I'm going to introduce a matrix to help you decide which options fit which situations. Then, I'm going to state the prospect's preferences or needs to help you create options for that prospect. Here's the first scenario and the matrices for creating your options.

Let's assume that cash flow is the biggest concern this prospect has. Use the following three matrices (Tables 6.2 through 6.4) to help you create alternative packages. Simply circle or highlight your choice for each proposal item to create three options.

Table 6-2. Cash Flow Prospect – Option One

Dollar Amount	High	Requested	Low
Term	Longer	Typical	Shorter
Interest Rate	High	Typical	Low
Monthly Payment	High	Typical	Low
Collateral	More	Typical	Less
Personal Guarantees	Full guarantee	Limited guarantee	None
Security Agreements	Blanket security	Limited security	None

Table 6-3. Cash Flow Prospect – Option Two

Dollar Amount	High	Requested	Low
Term	Longer	Typical	Shorter
Interest Rate	High	Typical	Low
Monthly Payment	High	Typical	Low
Collateral	More	Typical	Less
Personal Guarantees	Full guarantee	Limited guarantee	None
Security Agreements	Blanket security	Limited security	None

Table 6-4. Cash Flow Prospect – Option Three

Dollar Amount	High	Requested	Low
Term	Longer	Typical	Shorter
Interest Rate	High	Typical	Low
Monthly Payment	High	Typical	Low
Collateral	More	Typical	Less
Personal Guarantees	Full guarantee	Limited guarantee	None
Security Agreements	Blanket security	Limited security	None

Here are the choices I made:

	Option One	Option Two	Option Three
Dollar Amount	Requested	Requested	Requested
Term	Longer	Longer	Longer
Interest Rate	High	Typical	Typical
Monthly Payment	Low	Low	Low
Collateral	Typical	More	Typical
Personal Guarantees	Full guarantee	Full guarantee	Full guarantee
Security Agreements	Blanket security	Limited security	Blanket security

What was the method to my madness? In option one, I assumed that the amount the prospect requested is the amount actually needed. I extended the term to lower the monthly payment, but this payment reduction was partially offset somewhat by the higher interest rate. The higher rate compensated me, the banker, for the risk associated with the longer loan term. Having said all that, the monthly payment is still lower than the payment would have been under the traditional loan term. From a security standpoint, I chose not to ask for more collateral. Instead I'm asking for a full personal guarantee and blanket security agreement.

Option two also assumes that the amount requested is the amount needed. Again, the term is extended. This time, however, I didn't raise the interest rate. I opted for more collateral, a full personal guarantee, and a limited security agreement to minimize my risk. The additional security allows me to reduce my risk, thereby reducing the risk compensation I need in the interest rate. Because I didn't raise the interest rate over what would typically be charged for this loan, the payment is lower than in option one.

The third option also uses the amount requested and the longer term. The interest rate is what I'd typically charge for "normal" loan conditions. This time, however, I'm hedging my risk by asking for a blanket security agreement instead of more collateral. You'll notice that in all instances I've asked for full personal guarantees. The reason is that a company experiencing cash flow problems is more likely to default on the loan; hence, I want the personal guarantees.

There's nothing magical about the choices I've made. There are a lot of alternatives that we could have created, probably more than either of us have identified. The key is that the options we've created balance what we give up to accommodate the prospects' needs with what we get in exchange. In the options I outlined I balanced a longer term with a higher interest rate, or more security, whether in the form of additional collateral, personal guarantees, or security agreement terms.

Let's change the prospects' focus from cash flow to interest cost. These prospects have plenty of cash; they simply want to keep their interest costs to a minimum. Circle or highlight the items you want to include in each option using Tables 6.5 through 6-7.

Table 6-5. Interest Cost Prospect – Option One

Dollar Amount	High	Requested	Low
Term	Longer	Typical	Shorter
Interest Rate	High	Typical	Low
Monthly Payment	High	Typical	Low
Collateral	More	Typical	Less
Personal Guarantees	Full guarantee	Limited guarantee	None
Security Agreements	Blanket security	Limited security	None

Table 6-6. Interest Cost Prospect – Option Two

Dollar Amount	High	Requested	Low
Term	Longer	Typical	Shorter
Interest Rate	High	Typical	Low
Monthly Payment	High	Typical	Low
Collateral	More	Typical	Less
Personal Guarantees	Full guarantee	Limited guarantee	None
Security Agreements	Blanket security	Limited security	None

Table 6-7. Interest Cost Prospect – Option Three

Dollar Amount	High	Requested	Low
Term	Longer	Typical	Shorter
Interest Rate	High	Typical	Low
Monthly Payment	High	Typical	Low
Collateral	More	Typical	Less
Personal Guarantees	Full guarantee	Limited guarantee	None
Security Agreements	Blanket security	Limited security	None

All right, let's compare notes. Here are my choices:

	Option One	**Option Two**	**Option Three**
Dollar Amount	Requested	Requested	Requested
Term	Shorter	Shorter	Shorter
Interest Rate	Low	Typical	Typical
Monthly Payment	High	High	High
Collateral	Typical	Typical	More
Personal Guarantees	Full guarantee	Limited guarantee	None
Security Agreements	Blanket security	Blanket security	Limited security

In all three options I've kept the loan amount as requested. The term has been shortened to help reduce interest costs. The shorter the term, the less total interest a borrower pays.

In option one, I also lowered the interest rate slightly because interest cost is so important to this prospect. To offset the additional risk and lower revenues, I'm asking for the usual collateral, full personal guarantee, and blanket security agreement. In option two, I'm not lowering the interest rate. I am, however, willing to give up some security in the form of limited personal guarantees in exchange for the higher interest rate.

In option three I kept the usual interest rate and offered an exchange of a limited security agreement and *no* personal guarantees for more collateral. As you can see, each of these options not only gives prospects the opportunity to achieve their primary goal—low interest cost—but a secondary choice in the form of the type of security they'd like to provide. These secondary choices make it easier for prospects to say "Yes" to our offerings.

We have one more prospect profile to address—prospects who are primarily concerned with the amount of security they provide to the bank. You know the drill. The matrices are included in Tables 6-8 through 6-10.

Table 6-8. Security Prospect – Option One

Dollar Amount	High	Requested	Low
Term	Longer	Typical	Shorter
Interest Rate	High	Typical	Low
Monthly Payment	High	Typical	Low
Collateral	More	Typical	Less
Personal Guarantees	Full guarantee	Limited guarantee	None
Security Agreements	Blanket security	Limited security	None

Table 6-9. Security Prospect – Option Two

Dollar Amount	High	Requested	Low
Term	Longer	Typical	Shorter
Interest Rate	High	Typical	Low
Monthly Payment	High	Typical	Low
Collateral	More	Typical	Less
Personal Guarantees	Full guarantee	Limited guarantee	None
Security Agreements	Blanket security	Limited security	None

Table 6-10. Security Prospect – Option Three

Dollar Amount	High	Requested	Low
Term	Longer	Typical	Shorter
Interest Rate	High	Typical	Low
Monthly Payment	High	Typical	Low
Collateral	More	Typical	Less
Personal Guarantees	Full guarantee	Limited guarantee	None
Security Agreements	Blanket security	Limited security	None

I'm sure that you're chomping at the bit to get my perspectives. Well, maybe it's more of a mild interest. Okay, you're thinking, "Frankly Scarlett, I don't give a ___!" Here they are anyway:

	Option One	**Option Two**	**Option Three**
Dollar Amount	Requested	Requested	Requested
Term	Typical	Shorter	Longer
Interest Rate	Higher	Higher	Higher
Monthly Payment	High	High	High
Collateral	Typical	Less	More
Personal Guarantees	None	Limited guarantee	None
Security Agreements	Limited security	Limited security	None

As you can see, I'm consistently charging a higher interest rate because I, as the banker, am taking on more risk as I'm asking for less security. The interest rate premium I charge in option one will be a little higher than in option two, because I'm shortening the term in option two. Option three's interest rate will be the highest of the three because this option carries the longest term. In each option I'm charging a premium interest rate over what I'd typically charge if I had the usual collateral, personal guarantee, and security agreements.

The monthly payment in all options will be higher than under "normal" conditions because the interest rates are higher than usual. Option three, where I'm also extending the loan term, might be the exception. If the numbers work out on option three and I can, indeed, offer a lower monthly payment than options one or two afford, I can give prospects a chance to make a lower monthly payment as a secondary choice, again making it more difficult for them to say "No."

What I'm giving up with the higher interest rates is security. In option one, I'm foregoing the personal guarantees and offering limited security agreements to get a higher interest rate. In option two, I'm trading less collateral for some personal guarantees. In option three I'm allowing the prospect to trade higher collateral for no personal guarantees and no security agreements.

Again, there are no right or wrong options. You can offer whatever bundles you choose. Over time, you'll get a greater sense for which options each type of prospect prefers and your bundles will take on a more consistent look and feel based on those preferences. That shouldn't, however, prevent you from tailoring bundles to various types of prospects. Remember, we only identified three borrower profiles here; there could be more. Within the realm of security alone, most prospects hate the personal guarantee, are ambivalent toward the security agreement, and are cautious about the collateral they pledge. Yet there are those who, like yours truly, feel that the blanket security agreement has greater potential to limit future borrowing than the personal guarantee. Developing a separate set of options for these borrowers makes sense.

There's another opportunity that I see for bankers to increase the options available to their prospects. If you recall, I said at the beginning of this example that commercial banks typically keep their lending and deposit activities under separate umbrellas. That's due, in part, to the vast array of deposit programs available and the complexity of the regulatory aspects of lending. If bankers used a team approach in selling—if their loan officers and cash management people worked together on the sales call—they could build various cash management program benefits into the total bundle and really distinguish themselves from their competitors. Imagine that you're a borrower and you're trying to decide on loan offerings from three different banks. One banker offers the traditional take-it-or-leave-it option. A second banker's proposal offers three loan options. The third banker's proposal not only offers you several loan options, but shows you how their cash management programs can offset your borrowing costs. Which are you likely to choose?

The number and types of options that we can offer are limited only by our creativity. My experience is that the more options you create, the more creative you become. That's why I've built so many examples into these chapters. The keys to avoiding "No" to closing the sale are:

1. Offering options; as obvious as this seems, some businesspeople don't offer options.
2. Clearly delineating the options and the value each provides.
3. Pricing each option to assure higher levels of customer satisfaction.
4. Deciding whether to sell up or sell down; that is, do you start with the low price option or the high price option?

Now that you have the tools to increase your close rate in sales calls, let's see how we can use what we've learned to bring more prospects in the door. That's our goal in Chapter 7.

Executive Summary

1. While we want to graciously walk away from customers who don't value what we offer, we want increase the sales close rate on those who do.
2. Offering options reduces the likelihood that a prospect will say "No," because well-constructed options educate buyers and consider their budget needs.
3. The keys to creating effective options are:
   • Offering options; as obvious as this seems, some business-people don't offer options.
   • Clearly delineating the options and the value each provides.
   • Pricing each option to assure higher levels of customer satisfaction.
   • Deciding whether to sell up or sell down; that is, do you start with the low price option or the high price option?
4. Selling down, starting with a higher-priced offering and working your way down to the lower-priced options increases the likelihood of closing the sale

CHAPTER 7

Value as a Marketing Tool: Attracting the Right Buyers

A friend of mine asked me to review the changes she'd made to her Web site. The site touted an impressive array of benefits that her customers would get from her offerings. The power of these benefits evaporated when she said used the "A" word—affordable.

When I suggested that her marketing script and pricing sent conflicting messages to the market, she said "But affordable is one of the key words I found in my SEO (search engine optimization) search."

You know me well enough by now to know I wasn't buying that argument. You also know that I rarely tell people what they need to know. Instead, I ask them questions, à la Chapter 4, and allow them to discover the answers themselves. In this case, I asked my friend, "Is your goal to get a large number of hits or hits from people who are really interested in what you offer?" To her credit, she found a way to continue to use the word "affordable" without diminishing the value of her offerings. She accomplished this by defining affordable as a pricing guarantee—a guarantee that stated the customer would never be billed for cost overruns.

Unfortunately, my friend's *initial* approach to marketing is a common occurrence. You don't have to trust me on this. Simply recall ads that you have seen on television, heard on the radio, or read in print. Can you recall any that didn't tout low price as part of the message? If you can, I'll bet that you can count them on the fingers of one hand . . . and I'm not a betting man.

I won't belabor this point because we've discussed it in earlier chapters, but it's worthy of brief mention—low price is not a significant factor in *value-buyers'* decisions. Since our goal is to help you get higher prices so that you're compensated well for the value you provide, we need to find ways for you to attract those buyers who value what you offer and are willing to pay a premium to get it.

The keys to attracting the right buyers are:

1. Understanding the value you provide.
2. Crafting messages that have meaning for your buyers.
3. Using language that conveys your value.
4. Avoiding price language that diminishes the value you provide.
5. Creating an effective call to action.

Let's take a look at each of these in the order they're presented to see why they're so essential to your ability to get higher prices.

Attracting the Right Buyers

The first key to attracting ideal buyers is to understand the value you provide. If you don't understand that value, you can't possibly communicate it effectively. Let's see what's involved in understanding your offerings' value and how that fits into your marketing messages.

Understanding the Value You Provide

Value is perceived by many as a subjective judgment. Many buyers infer value from the price of the offering—a high price indicates high quality, a low price suggests low quality. It's the old "you-get-what-you-pay-for" adage that we're taught as we grow up. Hopefully I've dispelled that myth by demonstrating that buyers often get much more than they pay for because most sellers don't know how to quantify value.

Fortunately, you're no longer among this group. You learned to quantify the value of your offerings in Chapter 3. But old habits die hard. You're in the habit of talking about low or affordable prices. It's going to be tough to resist the temptation to use that language again. You must resist, though, if you ever expect to be paid well for the value you provide. That brings us back to the purpose of this section: understanding the value you provide.

What value do you provide? As I said at the beginning of this section, for many people value is a subjective judgment that lies in the eyes of the beholder. What you feel is valuable may have little or no interest to your customers. Yet there are inevitably things about your offerings that your customers prize highly, and you may not be aware of them. This was certainly true for me. I was absolutely convinced that the value I brought to my customers came from the breadth of my business experience in a variety of industries and my ability to get results. In reality, what they valued most was the discipline I brought into their lives—the fact that I helped them stay focused on what was of greatest importance in their businesses.

Are you making the same mistake I did? Are you making assumptions like I did? If so, stop it! Take a few minutes to survey your customers to see what it is that they truly value. Ask them, "If you had to pick one or two things that you enjoy most about our offerings or make your life easier, what would they be?" This question generally works better in face-to-face meetings with your customers than in an on-line or paper survey. In person, you can sense the genuineness and power of their comments. If there is passion and excitement in their voices, you know that you have a legitimate value proposition—one that you can incorporate into your marketing messages. On the other hand, if they're making something up to appease you, be gracious and thank them for their feedback, then ignore it. It has little value.

Pay particular attention to the language your customers use in answering the survey questions. You'll want to incorporate that language into your marketing messages. Don't forget to ask whether you can use their comments in a testimonial. If they agree, take what they said and put it into testimonial format and let them review it prior to using it in your marketing materials. Drafting the testimonial for them makes it easier for them to say "Yes" to your requests. It also assures that you have the opportunity to create congruity with other aspects of your marketing messages.

Before we move on, let's reiterate the key to this section: you need to understand value *from the customers' perspective*. What you think is irrelevant; it's your customers' perspectives that count.

Crafting Messages That Have Meaning for Your Buyers
Once you know what your customers value, communicating that value is pretty straightforward, right? Oh, if life were that simple. The reality

is that while most of your customers will value the same two or three things about your offering, they don't value them equally. One group of customers may value convenience over image or dependability, while a second group may be so obsessed with image that convenience isn't even on the radar screen. A third group may prefer dependability for its budget implications. They believe that dependable products tend to last longer and require fewer repairs, thereby saving them money. What implications does this have for you in crafting your marketing messages?

Obviously, one message doesn't fit all. You're going to need an array of messages, each with a different primary value statement. Let's say that your survey indicated that your customers value (will pay a premium for) speed, friendliness, and quality. You'll need one set of marketing messages that tout speed, with friendliness and quality as *add-on* benefits. The second set of messages focuses on friendliness and places speed and quality in the support roles. Obviously, quality enters center stage with the third set of messages.

Some of you may be thinking that you'll confuse the market with this approach. It isn't true. You're not changing the value propositions in your messages; you're simply rearranging them to attract more buyers. The reason for this will become clear in a moment, as we discuss the need for a system to track the results of your marketing efforts.

You'll want to develop a tracking system that allows you to see which messages work best and for which customers. Let's say that you have a list of 1,000 potential prospects for your offerings. Your value propositions are speed, friendliness, and quality. Let's further assume that your first marketing message focuses on speed. You deliver your message to the 1,000 prospects, and you get a 10 percent return. If you establish a separate list (database) of these 100 prospects and label it in a way that indicates their primary interest is speed, you'll not only find it much easier to craft future marketing messages to these folks, you'll continue to enjoy a high response rate from them. Fail to track their preferences, and you run the risk of sending them messages that have no appeal to them. When that happens, you become a nuisance.

What about the other 900 prospects who didn't respond? Well, you now know that speed isn't all that important to them. That doesn't mean that they're not potential customers, just that speed doesn't hold as much value for them. What do you do next? You deliver a marketing message that emphasizes quality as the primary benefit, friendliness second, and speed third. We're not eliminating speed from the mix. That would be confusing. We're positioning speed as an additional benefit—a deal sweetener—to use the language from Chapter 5.

Once again, take the responses you get from the quality message, create a separate database, and label it "quality." That way you'll know that future messages to them should focus on quality first because that's what these buyers value most.

Repeat this process for any prospects who didn't respond to the first two messages. This time friendliness is focal point of the message, with quality and speed taking secondary roles. In reality, you have more than just three approaches, even though I've only suggested three in this discussion. Table 7-1 shows you the full range of combinations available to you.

Some of you may be thinking, "Wait a minute, Dale! I don't have time to create all of these different messages, much less do the tracking you're suggesting. Besides, it would cost a bloody fortune to run that many messages with any regularity." I'm happy to report that both concerns are easily overcome.

We are blessed to live in a time when relatively inexpensive computer software exists that:

- Automatically delivers our marketing messages according to the schedules we set.
- To prospects we've identified.
- With customized messages tailored to their needs.
- Allows us to track the response rates we get.
- Helps us segment our database on the basis of these responses.

These tools dramatically reduce the amount of time and energy you need to spend delivering your marketing messages and tracking the responses. This allows you more time to craft messages that capture the prospect's interest and generate more sales.

Hopefully, we've dealt with your concerns about time, although we haven't addressed your fear of a runaway marketing budget. To deal with this concern, I'm going to refer you to Jay Abraham's book, *Getting Everything You Can Out of All You've Got.*[12] Mr. Abraham's solution? Test! In our example of 1,000 prospects, he'd tell us to deliver our messages to 10

Table 7-1. Marketing Message Options for Speed, Quality, and Friendliness

	Primary Value	*Secondary Value*	*Sweetener*
Option 1	Speed	Quality	Friendliness
Option 2	Speed	Friendliness	Quality
Option 3	Quality	Friendliness	Speed
Option 4	Quality	Speed	Friendliness
Option 5	Friendliness	Quality	Speed
Option 6	Friendliness	Speed	Quality

or 20 prospects at a time, and then see what response we get. Refine your message; test again. Repeat the process until you're getting the response rates you're seeking. Jay Abraham's approach helps you minimize your marketing costs while you hone your messages.

Once again, the keys to crafting effective marketing messages are:

- Using what you learned from your customer surveys about what they value.
- Putting those value propositions into your messages using your customers' language.
- Mixing those elements of value in ways to discern what's most important to each of the buyers your message targets.
- Making sure that all follow up messages to buyers emphasize the element of value that's most important to them.

Now that we know what's involved in crafting a message, let's see how the language we use influences buyers' perception of value.

Using Language That Conveys Your Value

There are typically two approaches that business owners use in communicating the value of their offerings. Either they use superlatives like "#1, world-class, blue-ribbon, and best," to describe their offerings. Or they keep the "hype" out of the message in the belief that their offerings will speak for themselves. Neither approach works very well. Buyers tend to discount claims companies make about their own offerings. The greater the claim, the more skeptical buyers become. Conversely, a subdued marketing message leaves buyers wondering why they should get excited about an offering when the company, itself, isn't.

There is a third mistake that many, many companies make in crafting their marketing messages—they talk about what they do, not what their customers get. Marketing firms tell you that they help you identify your ideal prospects, develop a system to get your salespeople in front of those prospects, and save your salespeople time. They tell you everything but what you want to know. You want to know how much additional revenue they can help you generate. That's the only thing you really want to know, right?

It's not my intent to pick on marketing firms. Manufacturers do the same thing. Does this sound familiar? "We have a one-of-a-kind process that streamlines throughput, increases productivity, and saves you money." Are those the things you really want? Of course not! You want to beat the pants off your competitors. You want to outperform them on the production side of your operation so that you can attract their customers.

What about the health club that advertises "state-of-the-art equipment, a custom program to meet your specific needs, and well-trained staff to guide you through the program." Do you want state-of-the-art equipment? Do you want a custom program? Do you want to work with trained staff? I doubt it. You probably want to lose 20 pounds so that you can look and feel younger and healthier. The question is, "How do you avoid these missteps?"

The key lies in the language you use. The language must be:

- Customer focused.
- Results oriented.
- Exciting.
- Appropriate for the value provided.

Customer-Focused Language
The message needs to speak to customers' needs. Enterprise Rent-A-Car built its business with the marketing message, "We pick you up." This simple sentence captures the essence of what their customers want. They want to avoid the hassle of jockeying schedules to pick up a rental

car. Enterprise expands this message to remind customers of the various situations that might cause them to want to be picked up. Situations that involve auto accidents, cars breaking down, cars not starting, and vehicles needed to carry a larger load or for a long trip.

Enterprise ads focus exclusively on customers' needs for convenience, not on the system Enterprise uses, the way it's staffed, or how it's able to provide this service and price itself competitively. None of these things are discussed in its ads. Why? Because Enterprise knows that its customers don't care about those things. All they want to know is that they're going to be picked up with the rental car of their choice when they want it. That's all they care about. Your marketing messages need to follow this model—touting what customers get instead of what you provide.

Results-Oriented Language

If you are able to quantify the results that your customers can expect, then do it. When you have a product that saves homeowners 20 percent on their heating and air-conditioning bills, provide testimonials to support that. If your investment strategies limit your client's downside risk to 6 percent during economic downturns, show results comparisons.

What do you do when you don't have measureable results? Use language that lets the customer gauge the value themselves. Enterprise doesn't, to my knowledge, make any claims as to the dollar value of its courtesy pick up; the ads simply show examples of stressful situations and allow the customer to evaluate its value to them knowing that stress increases perceived value. When you're feeling stressed, money is not an issue; you just want to be rid of that stress.

In Chapter 6, we used this indirect method of ascribing value in our home theater system example. Let's revisit the language we used:

Bose top-of-the-line system	"For those who want the ultimate experience in sight and sound and those who want only the best."
Samsung top-of-the-line system	"For discerning listeners and viewers looking for high quality at an affordable price"
Sony entry-level system	"For occasional users and starter budgets who demand quality and dependability"

First, I'd like you to notice that these messages are all customer focused—they meet the first language criterion we identified. There isn't one word in the messages above that describes the systems, their components, or anything about the company that sells them. Instead, these messages focus on the customer and what they want.

Second, the language is results oriented; it *implicitly* describes the experience (the result) customers can expect. Bose buyers can expect "the ultimate experience," but the message leaves the definition of "ultimate" to buyers for their interpretation. Samsung buyers are "discerning listeners," again, without defining the term "discerning." There aren't any specifics in these statements, yet buyers sense that the experience will be dramatically better with the Bose system.

Finally, even with the Sony entry-level model, buyers are going to get "quality and dependability." As you can see, even in something as esoteric as sight-and-sound experiences, we can convey the result without quantifying it. The more clearly your language helps buyers see the results they'll get, the more revenue you'll generate.

Exciting Language

Don't forget that people buy on emotion, and then justify their purchases with logic. Even when you have measurable results, don't focus just on the metrics. Focus on what opportunities that result affords. Let's go back to the heating and air-conditioning example I used earlier in this section. Your product typically saves homeowners 20 percent on their utility bills. Is that really what customers want? All of us enjoy saving money, but does saving money prompt them to buy? Not for most of us. If we were really excited about saving money, then we'd all have insulating blankets around our water heaters and adequate insulation in our attics.

If, however, the marketing message reminds these buyers that those savings could be used to buy a new car, remodel the kitchen, upgrade their hotel during their next vacation, or allow them to afford another meal at their favorite restaurant, their interest in saving money goes up dramatically. It's the emotional appeal of what they want that drives their desire to save money.

There are other ways that language can excite the buyer. Humor is a great way to get buyers' attention and spark their desire to buy. Humor, though, is a two-edged sword. While it can cut through all of the marketing noise and grab buyers' attention, it also has the potential to offend. The safest form of humor is self-deprecation. When you make fun of yourself or your offerings, people feel more comfortable. Here's a brief example.

My dad was an automotive mechanic. I often tell buyers that I didn't inherit that gene and relate a story of how I screwed up a fairly simple household repair. I end the story by telling them, "that's why I do what I do for a living."

This simple technique lets buyers know that I'm human—that I, too, have limitations. My acknowledgment of my limitations implicitly lets them know that I'm not going to think less of them because their backgrounds are limited in some areas. The fact that I've been honest with them about my limitations gives them confidence in what I say. They also sense that I'm confident in my ability to be successful in my chosen field—business. It's counterintuitive, but poking fun at yourself or what you offer enhances buyers' comfort and confidence. By all means use the language of humor in your marketing messages, but direct the humor at yourself or your offerings to avoid offending prospective buyers.

Another way to generate excitement with your offering is to target buyers' pain. There is no greater urgency that people feel than the need to rid themselves of pain. This reality isn't limited to physical pain, such as headaches, backaches, and arthritis. Being shy can be painful. Lacking the confidence to make decisions induces stress that can be both emotionally and physically painful. Feeling trapped in a job that you don't like is painful.

If you have ways to help people avoid, minimize, or eliminate pain, you can expect quick action as long as your language accurately describes the pain buyers are experiencing and your solution sounds plausible. It's the reason why pharmaceutical companies advertise to consumers. They know that people in pain are going to ask their doctors about the remedies they see on television. If you want buyers' excitement to translate into quick action, use language that targets their pain.

A third way to generate excitement is by targeting buyers' dreams. It is the least likely of the three—humor, pain, or dreams—to get buyers to act quickly. Why? In part because buyers' know that it often takes years for dreams to become reality. They're also easily distracted by the challenges of daily living, leaving them little time to spend dreaming or working on their dreams. If you want to overcome these obstacles, your marketing language has to show buyers' how they can make that dream come true "Today!" with little effort on their part.

If I were to rank these three language alternatives in terms of their ability to generate excitement, I'd rank pain first, humor second, and dreams third. The prospect of eliminating pain is very exciting. Who among us doesn't reach for the aspirin bottle as the first sign of a headache? Few of us choose to endure pain when there is a remedy readily available.

I ranked humor second for several reasons. One is that humor is one of the first things to go when people are experiencing pain. People in pain are naturally cranky and often resent those around them who are having fun. Humor won't appeal to these folks until the pain is gone.

Another reason is that, for people who are pain free when they hear your message, humor is more exciting than dreams. Humor is something they can experience and enjoy *now* with little or no effort on their part. All they have to do is place themselves near someone who is having fun, you, and they'll have fun, too. It's a whole lot easier than working on a dream.

Finally, the language of dreams is the least exciting because buyers quickly realize that your offering is only part of the solution in realizing that dream. Here are a few dreams I might have and the thought process that I would go through as a buyer.

I want to experience the fun and excitement of owning a Ferrari, and then I realize how much of my budget it requires. I really want that promotion, and then I realize that I'd have to get a Ph.D. to qualify. I want the ultimate experience of that Bose top-of-the line system, until I realize that there are other dreams I'd like fulfilled as well and that they, too, require money.

As you can see, there are several ways to generate excitement in your offering. They are not, however, equal in their ability to get buyers act quickly.

Appropriate Language for the Value Provided
Don't set unreasonable expectations with your offerings. Nothing diminishes the long-term profit potential of a customer like unfulfilled promises. Let's return to our home theater system exercise to get a sense

of appropriate language. For the Bose system, we used the phrase "ultimate experience"; for Samsung we used "discerning listener." There is a palpable difference between "ultimate" and "discerning." If we had been less careful in our choice of words, we might have said that the Samsung system provided "an incredible sight-and-sound experience at an affordable price." Which part of the message do you remember, "incredible sight and sound" or "affordable"? Most buyers would recall "affordable," which means that their focus is now on price rather than the experience they'll get.

What about "incredible sight and sound"? Does it make it easier or more difficult for you to decide which system fit your needs? Would you expect the quality of the Samsung system to be close to that of the Bose system? If so, what would you think when you listened to both and experienced a significant difference between the two? What would you think of the seller who used that language? Would you feel that the seller is honest? Would you feel confident taking the seller's advice? How likely would you be to buy from this person? That's how your buyers will feel about you if your language doesn't accurately describe the value your offering affords.

Overstating value leads to skepticism, distrust, and lost revenues. Understating value diminishes buyer excitement for the offering and, again, risks losing the sale. Appropriate value statements heighten buyer confidence which makes it easier for them to buy. Now that we've determined how to use language appropriately to convey value, let's make sure we don't give away that value with the rest of the message.

Avoiding Price Language That Diminishes the Value You Provide

Words and phrases like "lowest price around," "affordable," "good value for the dollar," "guaranteed low prices," and "at a fair price" leave buyers with the impression that they're giving something up. They don't know what, but they're giving something up because they're getting a low price.

The vast majority of buyers expect to pay more when the value is higher. Thus, a marketing message touting great value creates an expectation of a higher price. When a subsequent part of the message indicates a lower than expected price, it creates confusion for buyers. They wonder, "Am I really getting great value or am I being lured into a low-price purchase with false promises? If the value is as great as they claim, how can they afford to sell for such a low price?" Confusion spawns indecision. Buyers faced with conflicting language will usually walk away from a purchase before they'll invest time and energy trying to figure out which is more accurate, the value statement or the price.

You can avoid this dilemma by simply using price language that is congruent with the value of your offering. There is a sales training firm in St. Louis that advertises the fact that its training is expensive and explains why it is so. An asphalt paving company's message says: "We're not the most expensive, nor are we the cheapest. We provide quality at a fair price." Even though "fair price" is a phrase I cautioned against using, in this situation it makes sense because it reinforces the company's position of not having the highest or lowest price. It's also congruent with its claim of "quality." The ad didn't say great quality, superior quality, or affordable quality—just quality. This implied that the quality was commensurate with the price. The marketing message is congruent with the price language. That's the key to avoiding the use of pricing language that diminishes the value you established in the early part of your marketing message.

The fifth and final step in attracting the right buyers' is a call to action.

Creating an Effective Call to Action

An effective call to action is an often-overlooked part of the marketing message. You can get everything else right—you can clearly understand the value you provide, craft messages that have meaning to buyers, use language that conveys your value, and avoid price language that diminishes the value of your offerings—and yet fail to generate more revenues because you don't have a call to action. Without it, many buyers think, "Wow, I like this (your offering)! I'll have to remember to get (your offering) next week." Unfortunately, the memory of your message gets lost as life brings your buyers new challenges to address.

How do you avoid losing sales to buyers' short-term memories? Frequency is one solution. The more often they hear your message, the less likely they're to forget it. Of course, this approach doesn't help shorten the cycle from marketing message to sale. That's what we're really seeking.

A better approach is to take a play from retailers' playbooks—create urgency. While I often rail at retailers for discounting their offerings early in their peak selling seasons, many are masterful at creating calls to action. They use phrases like "today only," "while supply lasts," "this weekend only," "from 2:00 to 5:00," or "for the first 100 buyers." These are calls to action that give buyers' reason to act *now*. Without them, buyers will wait until it's *convenient* for them to act. Unfortunately, in today's fast-paced world, a "convenient" time rarely presents itself, which means that buyers don't quite get around to buying your offering. Their failure to act not only costs you in the form of lost sales, but in the loss of your marketing investment as well. Ouch! That's a one-two punch that really hurts.

Once again, its time to gain experience within the risk-free environment this book affords. The following exercises are designed to give you experience in creating and critiquing marketing messages. Enjoy!

Gaining Experience with Marketing Messages

Now that you have a sense of what it takes to attract the right buyers, let's give you a chance to gain some experience with these concepts. We'll use a couple of examples from earlier chapters to make life a little easier.

Horse Trainer: Attracting the Right Buyers

You may recall that our horse trainer only provided boarding as an accommodation to her customers. The boarding fees included everything necessary for the horse's health and safety—fly spray in the summer, blankets in the winter, regular exercise, and so on. This trainer's ideal customers were people who loved to *win* in hunter/jumper events; not just compete, but *win*. They are willing to pay for training for themselves and their horses. They also desire the convenience of having the trainer make the necessary reservations for these events, and they'd like to be able to budget for these costs. Using this information, craft a marketing message that will attract these buyers. Record your message in the space on the top of the next page.

Now, let's see whether or not you included all the elements identified above. Did your marketing message:

1. Demonstrate your knowledge of what the buyer values? If so, how?

2. Does the message have meaning to the customer? Which value attribute did your message emphasize? What other attributes could you have led with in your message?

3. Did your language demonstrate the value stated in your message or were buyers left to speculation on what the value was? Was the language you used customer focused, results oriented, and exciting? If you answered "no" to any of these questions, what would you change to improve your message?

4. Did you use any phrases that might have diminished the value of your value claims? If so, what were they? What language could you use instead?

5. What was your call to action? If you forgot one, what would your call to action be?

In the following paragraphs, I've created a sample message. Please review the message and critique it using the same questions you just used to evaluate your message. Space is provided below each question for your convenience in recording your comments. Here's the message I created:

"The (event name) hunter/jumper event, the most prestigious of the year, is just around corner. All of the best riders and horses will be there competing for first prize. While there's nothing like competing against the best to elevate your skills, *winning* against the best is the sweetest prize of all.

You and (horse's name) could win that prize, but you have to begin training now! We want to make sure that you peak just in time for the event. Timing is everything. Give me a call, and we'll schedule your training and make the necessary event reservations for you. Call now; you'll have first choice of available training times. Wait, and you may miss out completely. Demand for training for this event is always incredibly high. Don't be left out, call now at. . . . "

Again, list your comments in the space provided below each question. Did this message:

1. Demonstrate knowledge of what the buyer values? If so, how?

In this message, I chose to target the competitive nature of the rider. I could as easily have used a less prestigious event to appeal to relatively new riders or a third event designed for those with moderate skills. I could have used a gift-giving approach and asked the buyer to give the gifts of confidence and self-esteem that come from competing successfully. Similarly, I could have suggested that buyers' give themselves these gifts as a reward for themselves for the success they've enjoyed in other areas of the lives.

2. Does the message have meaning to the buyer? Which value attribute did the message emphasize? What other attributes could have led this message?

I believe that the references to competing, winning, prestige, and convenience all have meaning to these buyers. I could just as easily have led with convenience, but I don't think it has the same power that prestige and winning do.

3. Did the language demonstrate the value stated in the message or were buyers left to speculation on what the value was? Was the language used customer focused, results oriented, and exciting? If you answered "no" to any of these questions, what would you change to improve this message?

Did my language allow the buyer to experience the joy of winning and feel the pride of being a winner? If not, how can I elicit those emotions? Remember, all purchases are decided emotionally, then rationalized.

4. Were any phrases used that might have diminished the value of this offering? If so, what were they? What language could have been used instead? If you're struggling with these questions, begin with this question, "What price reference did this message include?" If none, what assumption did you make regarding price in the absence of a pricing reference?

If you were a current customer of this trainer, you might reasonably infer that the price for training would be the normal training fees. Prospects, on the other hand, wouldn't know what those training fees are, yet they would get the sense that they're not inexpensive. Why? The message talks about competing and winning against the best. You don't get to be the best without investing heavily in skill development.

The message also talks about the limited availability of training slots. Small supply and high demand always drives prices up. Implicit in the limited supply statement is the inference of a high price. These aspects of the message allowed me to communicate high value and an expectation of a high price. In other words, I believe that I achieved congruency between the value message and the pricing language.

5. What was the call to action? If it was forgotten, what would your call to action be?

You probably noticed that there were several calls to action embedded in this message. The first came in the first sentence of the second paragraph when I suggested that training should be started "now." The second came after I told them that we'd make reservations for them. The third came after I reminded them that there are limited training slots available. The fourth came immediately following the reminder that demand for training is always incredibly high for this event.

It's all right to have multiple calls to action. Actually, I recommend it. The key is to space them out a bit and change the language so that the calls are encouraging rather than annoying. Hopefully, I accomplished that goal.

Let's craft one more message. How about one for the clothier from Chapter 5.

Clothier: Attracting the Right Buyers

Many of the clothier's buyers suffer poor color memory, a lack of fashion sense, body shapes that don't match today's styles, short-term memory of what they have in their closets, and the challenge of buying clothes for others, including friends and family. After you craft your message, use the same questions as before. Here they are:

1. Demonstrate your knowledge of what the buyer values? If so, how?

2. Does the message have meaning to the customer? Which value attribute did your message emphasize? What other attributes could you have led with in your message?

3. Did your language demonstrate the value stated in your message or were buyers left to speculation on what the value was? Was the language you used customer focused, results oriented, and exciting? If you answered "no" to any of these questions, what would you change to improve your message?

4. Did you use any phrases that might have diminished the value of your value claims? If so, what were they? What language could you use instead?

5. What was your call to action? If you forgot one, what would your call to action be?

Let's compare notes. Here's the message I created:

> "Women, have you ever seen a blouse that's to die for only to find that it's made for a runway model instead of your curvaceous figure? Men, have you ever tried on a suit that makes you look like a tank when you were envisioning yourself as a jaguar? Stop fighting these battles! Come into (your store) today, and we'll help you find the right fashion for you.
>
> We have styles for all body shapes—styles that make you look as young as you feel, enhance the power of your already strong personality, highlight the wisdom you possess, and bring out your most attractive features. Come in today! Our fashion experts will help you select just the right style to bring out the best of who you really are.
>
> Don't forget, your clothes affect the way you feel. There's nothing more appealing than confidence whether you're looking for a life partner or trying to advance your career. Don't delay! You never know when that special someone or a new opportunity will present itself. Get started today. We're located at. . . ."

Once again, it's time for you to critique my message. Did I:

1. Demonstrate knowledge of what the buyer values? If so, how?

> Despite occasional denials, we human beings care about what others think. We want them to think highly of us. This value proposition is based on that knowledge. I build on that premise by reminding buyers that most of them don't really have a sense for what styles flatter their shapes and which detract from them rendering any choices they make questionable. It never hurts to build a little pain into the script.

2. Does the message have meaning to the customer? Which value attribute did the message emphasize? What other attributes could have been used in this message?

Have any of you had a really good friend (it takes a really good friend) tell you that something you're wearing makes you look dumpy, frumpy, or ridiculous? Most of us have. The fact that we've made fashion mistakes in the past is meaningful to buyers. Other value attributes I could have used include gift giving and the challenges that presents especially when there are generational differences, convenience in not having to return things, or budget constraints when the need for multiple outfits exist.

3. Did the language demonstrate the value stated in the message or were buyers left to speculation on what the value was? Was the language used customer focused, results oriented, and exciting? If the answer to any of these questions was "no," what language could be used to improve the message?

The references to life partners and career advancement give the sense that there can be a lot at stake. While the value isn't quantified in the marketing message, the value is implied in these references. The language was customer focused; it dealt with the challenges customers face in buying clothing. The results that buyers could expect are a truer or enhanced image and greater confidence. If I were to wordsmith this message some more, I believe that I could make it more exciting. I'd strive for language that helped buyers visualize themselves getting that promotion or finding the love of their lives.

4. Were there any words or phrases used that might have diminished the value of the value claims? If so, what were they? What language could I use instead?

Again, I didn't make any reference to price in the marketing message. The absence of price information makes sense given that my value attribute is image, because image buyers are accustomed to paying premium prices. If, however, I'd been targeting my message to budget-conscious buyers, I'd have used the mix-and-match approach to getting multiple outfits from fewer articles of clothing and said that they could get four outfits for the price of three. My intent was, once again, to draw upon buyers' natural presumption that pricing will be *fair* when price language is absent.

5. What was your call to action? If you forgot one, what would your call to action be?

Multiple calls appear in this message as well. How many did you count? There were four. There's nothing magical in that number. I recommend three to five calls to action in short marketing messages like those above and at least one more for each paragraph you add beyond that length.

We've just learned how to use value to attract the right buyers. Wouldn't life be grand if we could just keep pitching the same messages? Actually it would be really boring, not only for us, but our customers as well. While this need for change keeps life interesting, it also opens the door for missteps in the future. In Chapter 8, we'll see what traps await us, and how to avoid them.

Executive Summary

1. The keys to attracting the right buyers are:
   - Understanding the value you provide.
   - Crafting messages that have meaning for your buyers.

- Using language that conveys your value.
- Avoiding price language that diminishes the value you provide.
- Creating an effective call to action.

2. You need to understand value *from the customers' perspective.* What you think is irrelevant; it's your customers' perspectives that count.
3. When crafting marketing messages:

   - Use what you learned from your customer surveys about what they value.
   - Put those value propositions into your messages using your customers' language.
   - Mix those elements of value in ways to discern what's most important to each of the buyers your message targets.
   - Make sure that all follow up messages to buyers emphasize the element of value that's most important to them.

4. The language used in your marketing messages must be:

   - Customer focused.
   - Results oriented.
   - Exciting.
   - Appropriate for the value provided.

5. Customer-focused language talks about the result the customer wants to achieve, not what your company does or how it does it.
6. Results-oriented language can be, but doesn't have to be, measureable. Buying decisions are triggered by emotion, not by logic. Even when you have measureable results, the metrics used should be secondary to satisfying the buyers' emotional needs.
7. Language can be made more exciting by targeting buyers' pain, using humor, or tapping into their dreams. Of the three, pain is the most likely to get buyers to act quickly. We abhor pain. The second most likely is humor. Who among us doesn't enjoy being around people who like to have fun. Dream language is the least effective because we intuitively know that converting dreams to reality requires effort on our part.

8. Avoid giving away the value you build in the early part of your marketing messages by using price inferences like "lowest price around," "affordable," "good value for the dollar," "guaranteed low price," or "at a fair price." Your price language must be congruent with the value you communicate in the early part of your marketing message.

9. Take a tip from retailers and build multiple calls to action into your messages. If you don't create urgency, buyers will sit on the sidelines.

CHAPTER 8

The Value Trap: Avoiding the Pitfalls of Change

At the risk of stating the obvious, change is inevitable. In business, change can be categorized by source:

- Customer directed.
- Competitor directed.
- Self-directed.
- Technology directed.

We're going to explore each of these four types of change, highlighting the challenges each presents and the more common mistakes made in dealing with those challenges. Once we've accomplished that task, we'll establish a systematic approach for dealing with change regardless of its origin.

Identifying Pitfalls

As human beings we're creatures of habit. Whenever we're confronted by changes in our environment, especially unexpected changes, we return to old habits. With regard to pricing, that often means giving away value instead of being compensated for it. As we explore each of the types of change identified above, we're going to see exactly what these old habits are and how they're triggered. The goal is to help you avoid them in the future.

Customer-Directed Change

If you're lucky, really lucky, your customers will tell you what you need to do to improve your offerings. The reason I place such emphasis on luck is that, human nature being what it is, most customers suffer quietly with the deficiencies in your offerings (none of them are perfect, right?) until they find something better. Then, they switch and leave you wondering why you lost their business.

Let's assume that you're one of the lucky ones who have customers who tell you what improvements they'd like to see in your offerings. What are you going to do? You're going to make the improvements, right? Why would you ignore this gift from your customers? You may just have fallen into the first value trap.

If you recall from Chapter 3, we discussed the need to determine whether your customers' requests are merely conveniences they'd enjoy or improvements valuable enough that they're willing to pay extra to get them. If they're merely conveniences and you provide what they ask, you'll increase your costs without gaining any additional revenues. If that weren't bad enough, you've also given your customers reason to believe that you'll honor all future requests in the same manner: without any additional charge. Ouch! I'll bet you didn't see that one coming.

The key is to ask for compensation for each of the requests that customers make. In the second half of this chapter, we will discuss the specifics of how to do that. Before we do, let's take a look at the pitfalls associated with competitor-directed change.

Competitor-Directed Change

Most of us are pretty good at monitoring our competitors. We know what changes they're making to their offerings, with whom they're doing business, what their pricing is, in what ways their offerings are superior to ours, and in what ways our products and services outperform theirs. This approach leads you down a path to two easily overlooked traps.

The first is the natural inclination to match your competitors' offerings. Fear of losing competitive advantage can cause you to follow your competitors' leads without questioning the validity of that decision. If your competitors offer quicker turnaround times, you may feel compelled to do the same regardless of whether customers have requested it or are willing to pay for it. It's the incessant fear of losing business to your competitors that can drive you to make poor decisions as to whether or not to follow their lead. What's the alternative?

Instead of jumping on the bandwagon, you could research your customers' interest in the change your competitors are making, determine whether other aspects of your offering might overshadow the additional value competitors are offering, and analyze your competitors' business models to ascertain whether you're even targeting the same customer. If your competitors are using a low-price strategy and you're targeting image customers, there's no need to follow their lead. You have different business models!

The second trap that lies along the path of competitor-directed change is tunnel vision. We observe only those whom we feel are direct competitors. In doing so, we overlook those who are competing for the same dollars we are, but don't offer what we offer. In his book, *There's No Elevator to the Top,* Umesh Ramakrishnan relates the story of a Nestlé chairman who bemoaned the fact that he was no longer competing with the other candy companies, but with telecom companies. His customers, kids, were opting to spend their money on texting instead of sweets.[13]

One of the things you need to do to remain competitive is monitor the spending habits of your customers. That involves monitoring companies in "noncompeting" industries that target the same customers.

So far we've been dealing with change that's dictated by others. But we, too, have a desire to change. What traps lie along that path?

Self-Directed Change

One of the reasons you went into business for yourself is that you knew, absolutely knew, that your idea was better than anything else on the market. This innate desire to improve on what already exists doesn't go away just because you're offering a better mousetrap. You're destined to continue tinkering with your offerings to improve them.

Every time you find a way to improve your offering, your inclination is to go to market like a proud parent, proclaiming to the world the wonders of what you've created. Unfortunately, that's where the good news ends. In this process, you've overlooked a couple of value traps.

The first trap is one that most of us have fallen into, creating an "improvement" without first determining whether it's something our customers value. If it isn't, you're left with one of two options. You can either offer the "improvement" to your customers at no additional cost or you can withhold the "improvement" and lose the investment you made in creating it. Actually, the second alternative is the less expensive of the two options. Why? Because you incur additional costs every time that you provide the enhancement to your offering, but you don't gain any revenue to offset these costs. It's easy to overlook the ongoing costs that you'll incur in providing the "improvement" when you're facing the reality that you made a poor choice in deciding to create it in the first place.

The second trap that is often overlooked is your natural desire to use your improved offering as a way to create competitive advantage. You envision hoards of your competitors' customers shifting to you to take advantage of what you're offering. The reality is that there are many reasons why your competitors' customers have been loyal to them that have nothing to do with what you're offering. Buyers remain loyal to your competitors for many of the same reasons your customers remain loyal to you. They've become comfortable in dealing with you, they resist change, one of their relatives works for you, you did them a favor, and so on. These are some of the reasons why improved offerings seldom trigger significant shifts in customer buying habits. Yet we mistakenly give away the value we create in hopes that this time will be different.

When you give away your offerings' enhancement in an attempt to gain market share, you give away the revenues that you could have gained from your customers, those who do value the improvement, you forego the premium you would have gotten from competitors' customers who would have been willing to pay extra to get what you offer, and you send a message to the market that the improvement really isn't all that valuable. Ouch, ouch, ouch. The keys here are to make sure that your customers will pay extra for the changes you're envisioning *before* making the investment and to avoid the inclination to give away the improvement to gain competitive advantage.

We've got one category of change left, technology. Let's see what pitfalls it contains.

Technology-Directed Change

We live in an age when technology is changing at an incredible pace. In reality, that is true regardless of the era in which we live. I recall a passage from a book in which the character was amazed at how quickly news traveled thanks to the stagecoach and the telegraph. That was a real eye opener for me. To me, that passage says that the rate of technological change will always be amazing and somewhat overwhelming because of its newness. With that in mind, let's see what traps await us as we adapt to these changes.

The first technology trap lies in the belief that technology changes business principles. The tech bubble of 2000 is a classic example. If I were to begin the old joke "I know we're losing money, but we're going to make it up in _____," you'd easily fill in the blank with the word "volume." Yet many tech companies felt that if they developed a large enough following they'd be able to attract advertisers to make them profitable. In other words, they were counting on volume to make them profitable. The friend I cited in Chapter 7 was initially interested in getting a lot of hits on her Web site instead of targeting those buyers who value what she offers. What's the lesson here? Before employing new technology, make sure that it supports a business model you know works.

The second technology trap involves implementation. As an early adopter of technology, you can gain a competitive advantage *if* your customers share your enthusiasm for technology. If that isn't the case, make sure that you choose a rate of adoption that fits your customers' profile. In Chapter 4, we categorized innovation buyers as early adopters, dependability buyers, and late adopters. Assuming that you, like most business owners, have customers who fit all three profiles, you should have one version of your offering for early adopters, those customers who share your proclivity for new things, a second for dependability buyers who enjoy technology only when it's proven, and a third version for those who won't adopt the new technology until they have no other choice. The keys here are to test new technology with those early adopters to see whether or not it has value to them, offer it to dependability buyers when the technology is proven, and finally stop offering the old technology when it becomes too costly to maintain. That will force the late adopters to change.

Now that we've identified the more common pitfalls you face in dealing with change, let's develop a systematic approach for avoiding them.

Avoiding Pitfalls

It would have been easy to end this chapter with the suggestions listed above, but I know from experience that those suggestions would be of little help to you. Why? Because, as mentioned earlier, we're creatures of habit. We get caught up in the daily challenges of running a business and quickly forget the advice of this chapter. To minimize that risk, I've developed a four-step system that, if you employ it will help you avoid giving away the value you create. Here is the system:

1. If you don't have a board of directors, either get one, use one of the myriad companies that provide quasiboards of directors for noncompeting companies, or create a mastermind group (a group of three to five people dedicated to helping one another be successful in their respective businesses). You can learn more about mastermind groups in Napoleon Hill's book, *Think and Grow Rich.*[14] The goal is to have people who aren't members of your industry, but are successful in their own industries, help you react appropriately to the changes you face.

2. Meet once a month with your board of directors, quasiboard, or mastermind group. Near the top of the agenda, list each the four categories of change, along with the changes you face in each category. That way you won't forget to discuss them with people who are capable of giving you an external perspective on each of these changes.

3. Make sure that members of the senior leadership team within your organization are aware of the contents of this chapter. If you don't have a senior leadership team, chose two or three people in your organization on whom you can count for candor and valuable insights to share this information. Next, charge them with the responsibility of challenging you any time they

see you moving toward any of the traps identified in this chapter. If you have weekly, biweekly, or monthly meetings with these people, again, make sure the agenda includes time for the changes that you, and they, see occurring from any of these sources.

4. During the discussion of the changes you're facing, whether in the board meeting or with your leadership team, make sure that these questions are being asked:

- For customer-requested changes, are our customers willing to pay for them? If so, how much? What investment will we have to make to address this change? Is the payback great enough to make the investment?

- For direct competitors' changes, are we targeting the same customers? Are our business models really that similar? Are the changes our competitors are offering that valuable to our customers? If they are and we find that we must match their offering to remain competitive, how do we rebundle our offerings to assure that we're compensated for the additional value? If the changes aren't really valued by our customers, how can we show them that other aspects of our offerings outweigh the new "benefit" our competitors are touting without denigrating the competition?

- For indirect competitors' changes, which companies outside our industry are targeting the same customers we are? What impact will their offerings have on our future revenues? How can we attract more revenue dollars from their customers?

- For self-directed changes, have we surveyed our customers to see whether they're willing to pay for the enhancements? If not, what would make their lives easier, more enjoyable, and their work more profitable? What are they willing to pay for these improvements? Do we have the ability to provide what they desire? What investment would we have to make? What's the payback on that investment?

- For technology changes, how does this technology support our business model? How can we use this new technology to enhance the value our customers receive? Are they willing to pay for the additional value? Is what they're willing to pay adequate for the investment we have to make? For those that are willing to pay, how can we accommodate them while not disturbing the relationships we have with dependability buyers and late adopters?

As you can see, the methodology I've proposed is simple and consistent. The keys are getting outside input, keeping awareness of the pitfalls of change fresh in your and your leadership's minds, and making conscious rather than reactive decisions to the changes you face.

Now that you have an approach for dealing with changes that you face on a regular basis, let's take a look at changes that occur less frequently, changes in the economy. That's our focus in Chapter 9.

Executive Summary

1. There are four categories of change:

   - Customer directed.
   - Competitor directed.
   - Self-directed.
   - Technology directed.

2. Regardless of the source of change, the methodology for avoiding value traps includes:

   - Engaging an outside board of directors or its equivalent.
   - Meeting regularly with that board or its equivalent.
   - Meeting regularly with your leadership team.
   - Setting your board and leadership meeting agenda so that the changes you're facing are addressed early in the meeting.

CHAPTER 9

The Economy:
It Just Doesn't Matter!

Inspiration can be found in the most unlikely places. The inspiration for the title of this chapter came from the movie, *Meatballs*.[15] In the movie, Bill Murray plays camp counselor for a rag-tag group of misfits. The annual contest between his camp and the "in-crowd" camp across the lake is to be held the next morning. His camp has lost for the past dozen years. Murray's "pep talk" lists all the reasons why his kids are likely to lose and why the other camp will win. During his speech he repeats the phrase, "It just doesn't matter!" He repeats it so often that the kids take up the chant, eventually realizing that the result of the contest isn't as important as they think it is. That's the message I'd like to convey to you. The economy isn't as important as you think it is.

Why the Economy Doesn't Matter

I'm sure that some of you are thinking about tossing this book into the round file. Don't! At least wait until you've heard my rationale. Here are the reasons why I say that the economy doesn't matter.

1. *In any economy, some businesses will thrive while others suffer.* Here's a quick example. When interest rates are low, people buy big-ticket items, such as homes and cars. Homebuilders and car dealers make money despite themselves in this economy, while home remodelers and auto repair shops struggle. Conversely, when interest rates are high, it's the homebuilders and car dealers that suffer. What's the message here? Just because your "tra-

198

ditional" market is struggling doesn't mean there aren't other markets for you to serve.

Whether you're selling business to business or business to retail, there are buyers who are flourishing. Identify those buyers, market to them, and you, too, will flourish. How do you do this?

If you're a homebuilder in a high-interest-rate economy, target wealthy buyers whose homes reflect their image, who want to enhance that image during difficult times, and who can afford high-interest rates. As an alternative, you can target renters who are looking for a way to build equity, even if it's in a small home. You can help them make the transition from renter to home owner.

If you're an auto-repair shop owner and you're facing a low-interest-rate economy, an economy in which buyers are more likely to buy a new car than repair their old one, tout maintenance programs that are designed to protect their new investments.

2. *People will pay extra for what they really want regardless of the economy.* Indeed, things like quality and dependability have greater value when money is tight. Why? Because even cost-conscious buyers realize that spending a little more now for quality can save them money in the future.

In addition, buyers who have been successful and created an image of success in good economies will pay extra to maintain that image, even when they find the current economy challenging.

And finally, some buyers will forego eating out to be able to afford their dream trip. Others will postpone the trip to be able to eat out. Buyers will make adjustments in their spending habits, but they will spend, and handsomely, for the things they really value. Wouldn't you splurge on that dream vacation if you just spent six months foregoing dinners at your favorite restaurants?

3. *Buyers' natural styles don't change just because the economy does.* Value buyers will always be value buyers, just as price buyers will always be price buyers. Price buyers will be looking for the best deal they can get *even when* they're rolling in money. Value buyers, on the other hand, will forego some purchases during difficult times rather than sacrifice the things they value.

4. *The rules of bundling apply to all economies.* In Chapter 5, the rules we outlined apply equally well in good and bad economies. Those value buyers mentioned in number three above, the ones who might postpone purchases, may be enticed to buy earlier if you offer a bundle that provides slightly less value, but with a commensurately lower price.

   Bundles aren't meant to be static. They're, by nature, dynamic because they need to adapt to the wide array of changes outlined in Chapter 8. Their dynamic nature makes them ideal for helping you adjust to changing economies.

5. *You don't always have to change the bundle to deal with changing economies.* In Chapter 7, we learned about the power of language in attracting buyers. If you employ language well in your marketing messages, you won't have to change your offering or its price. Here's an example:

   One of my training programs, *Making the EXCEPTIONAL Normal,* is designed to help managers improve the productivity of their work force *and* create a work environment that allows them to attract high-caliber talent.

   In economies where unemployment is high, my marketing message says "I know that you need more people to meet all the demands on your team, but you don't have the budget to hire them. The *Making the EXCEPTIONAL Normal* program is designed to help your team achieve its goals with less stress and help you stay within budget."

   When unemployment is low, my message is "I know that you need more people to meet all the demands on your team, but there simply isn't good talent available today. The *Making the EXCEPTIONAL Normal* program is designed to help your team achieve its goals with less stress and help you avoid the hassle and high costs of dealing with people who don't fit your needs."

   I'm offering exactly the same program with the same pricing. All I did was adapt my marketing message to the economy the buyers were facing. When you're able to make this kind of adjustment in your marketing messages, does the economy really matter?

Hopefully you've decided to hang onto this book. I'm not denying the fact that from time to time each of us inevitably enjoys economic bliss and suffers the pinch of economic downturns. Indeed, as I'm writing this chapter in late February 2009, people globally are experiencing some of the most far-reaching economic challenges in 80 years.

It's not my intent to make light of these trying circumstances. Instead, my goal is to provide all of you who are experiencing economic downturns, whenever they may hit, with the tools to minimize their impact on you, your business, and your customers *without* lowering prices. What do you do if all of your competitors are lowering their prices?

The Right Way to Lower Prices

If you feel that must lower prices, then lower your offering as well. Lowering your price without getting commensurate concessions from your buyers leaves them with the following unanswered questions:

- "Was this seller getting into my knickers before? The offering didn't change, yet he or she can lower the price and remain profitable? Hmmm."
- "What did they change in the offering? Is the quality lower? Is it going to be less dependable? Has the quantity diminished (restaurants and food producers who reduce portion size are two examples of this approach)? Are they cutting back on service?"
- "Is the seller hurting so badly that they need to lower prices? If so, will they be around to provide service after the sale?

As you can see, none of these buyer impressions are favorable for the seller. If you want to avoid these perceptions:

- Don't lower your price without getting a concession from the buyer.
- If you're going to reduce some aspect of your offering, involve buyers in restructuring your bundles so that they know what they're giving up to get the price concession. If you simply insist upon rebundling your offerings without buyer input, at least no-

tify them in advance of what you're doing so that you don't appear duplicitous.

- If you want to instill confidence in your buyers, hold or raise your prices. After the 9/11 tragedy, many professional speakers were faced with an inordinately high rate of cancellations. Most of these speakers lowered their prices to salvage as many speaking dates as possible to little, if any, avail. A friend of mine took the opposite tack and raised her fees. She experienced growth in her revenues the following year. Why? She, in essence, told the market, "I'm good at what I do. I provide great value. I'm confident that we'll all weather these tragic events." People like to do business with people who are successful. What better way to demonstrate your success than holding, or better yet, raising your prices during difficult times?

As I close this chapter, Bill Murray's words echo in my mind, "It just doesn't matter! It just doesn't matter! It just doesn't matter!" Don't allow an economic downturn to cause you to abandon the precepts you've learned in this book. Use the tools you've been provided to help you avoid the mistakes that many business owners make: lowering prices without getting concessions from buyers.

In the next and final chapter, Chapter 10, I'll share my wish for you. On to Chapter 10!

Executive Summary

1. The economy doesn't matter because:

   - In any economy, some businesses are thriving while others suffer.
   - People will pay extra for what they really want regardless of the economy.
   - Buyers' natural styles don't change just because the economy does.
   - The rules of bundling apply to all economies.
   - You don't always have to change the bundle to deal with

changing economies; sometimes merely changing the marketing message is adequate.

2. If you feel that you must lower prices during an economic downturn:

   - Get buyer concessions before lowering your price.
   - Involve buyers in determining which concessions they're willing to make.
   - If you don't involve your buyers in determining concessions, at least communicate the changes you're making to avoid appearing duplicitous.

3. If you really want to send a positive statement to the market, raise or hold your prices when all others are lowering theirs'.

CHAPTER 10

Make More, Work Less

Very early in my consulting business, someone offered me this advice, "If you cut your fees in half, you can double your client base." Now I don't know about you, but working harder for the same amount of money doesn't have much appeal to me. Yet I see business owners working harder for less money every day. Some do it because they really do believe that bigger is better; others because they have the mistaken belief that low prices are the key to being competitive. Let's address both of these misconceptions.

Bigger Isn't Better

The bigger is better mentality isn't limited to small businesses. Juli Niemann, an economist and Chartered Financial Analyst with Smith Moore & Company in St. Louis, cites a First Chicago study of bank mergers and acquisitions. The study analyzed the impact of the mergers and acquisitions on banks' ratios and found that only one ratio went up, CEO salaries. The study showed that bank mergers weren't accretive; they did not add value except to the CEOs that ran them.

Please don't fall into the trap of growing for the sake of size. If you do, you will, indeed, work harder for less money. Why? The traditional growth approach many businesspeople take, in businesses large and small, involves lowering prices to acquire customers who don't necessarily value what they offer. If you use that approach, your costs will rise as your profit margins decline. It's a sure way to end up working harder for less money. Unlike the bank CEOs, your compensation won't go up just because you're running a larger company. Your compensation only goes up when you make more money. Hopefully I've dispelled the bigger is better myth. Now let's turn our attention to the misconception that low prices are necessary for a company to be competitive.

Avoiding Price Competition

For those of you who don't ascribe to the bigger is better philosophy, but are working too hard anyway, you *now* know the reasons why this has been happening. You also have the tools to enable you to make a lot more money with less effort in the future. These tools include:

- An understanding of how expensive low prices can be for you and your customers.
- Buyer profiles—being able to distinguish between price buyers and value buyers and use that information to create a profile of your ideal customer.
- Formulae for calculating value of your offerings.
- Scripts for helping your customers discover that value.
- Bundling to sweeten the deal for your customers *and* increase your profits.
- Options that improve your close rate once you've identified your ideal customer.
- Sample marketing messages that communicate value to your market.
- A methodology for dealing with the value traps associated with change.
- An understanding of why the economy "Just doesn't matter!"

My goal in providing this information is to help you make more money without working nearly so hard. My wish for you is that your business provides both the lifestyle you and your family desire and the time to enjoy it. I wish you tremendous success in achieving both goals.

Executive Summary

1. Bigger isn't necessarily better. The traditional growth approach many businesspeople take in large businesses and small involves lowering prices to acquire customers who don't value what they offer. The result is that business owners work harder for less money.

2. You have the tools to enable you to make a lot more money with less effort in the future. These tools include:

   • An understanding of how expensive low prices can be for you and your customers.
   • Buyer profiles—being able to distinguish between price buyers and value buyers and use that information to create a profile of your ideal customer.
   • Formulae for calculating value of your offerings.
   • Scripts for helping your customers discover that value.
   • Bundling to sweeten the deal for your customers *and* increase your profits.
   • Options that improve your close rate once you've identified your ideal customer.
   • Sample marketing messages that communicate value to your market.
   • A methodology for dealing with the value traps associated with change.
   • An understanding of why the economy "just doesn't matter!"

Notes

1. McKinsey & Company, *The War for Talent*. Boston: Harvard Business School Press, 2001.

2. *Wall Street Journal*, October 10, 2008

3. www.census.gov/cgi-bin/popclock

4. I did not include Chrysler stock, because Chrysler was owned by DaimlerChrysler during this period.

5. Jay Conrad Levinson, *Guerrilla Marketing*. Boston: Houghton Mifflin, 1984.
Now that we have revisited the definitions, let's begin.

6. Dale Furtwengler, *The Uniqueness Myth*. St. Louis, MO: Peregrine Press, 2004.

7. CEO, Jim Parker, quit after 3 years on the job. He cited fatigue from labor negotiations. *The Seattle Times*, July 16, 2004.

8. Jay Conrad Levinson, *Guerrilla Marketing*.Boston: Houghton Mifflin, 1984.

9. To simplify things and avoid the redundancy of saying customers and prospects repeatedly, I'm going to refer primarily to prospects throughout the remainder of this chapter even though the concepts apply equally well to customers and prospects. My rationale for focusing on prospects is that you have less familiarity with them than you do with your customers. In those instances that I do refer to customers, it's because the prospect has made the transition to customer or because I'm referring to your prospects' customers.

10. Robert B. Cialdini, *Influence: Science and Practice*, 4th ed. Boston: Allyn & Bacon, 2001, p. 21.

11. Robert B. Cialdini, *Influence: Science and Practice*, 4th ed. Boston: Allyn & Bacon, 2001, p. 21.

12. Jay Abraham, *Getting Everything You Can Out Of All You've Got*. New York: St. Martin's Griffin, 2000.

207

13. Umesh Ramakrishnan, *There's No Elevator to the Top*. New York: Portfolio (Penguin Group), 2008.

14. Napoleon Hill, *Think and Grow Rich*. Hawthorne, NY: JMW Group, 2003 and 2005.

15. *Meatballs*, Paramount Pictures, 1979.

Index

Index

About the Author

Dale Furtwengler is President of Furtwengler & Associates, P.C., a business consulting firm that helps clients *increase profits without adding resources*. One of the ways that Dale accomplishes this goal is by helping his clients quantify and communicate the value of their offerings. *Pricing for Profit* is designed to help you get compensated well for the value you provide. His work is recommended by the University of Glasgow, the University of New South Wales, and the Australian Institute of Management.

Among Dale's other publications are:

Making the EXCEPTIONAL Normal
The Uniqueness Myth and Other Misconceptions That Derail Businesses
The 10-minute Guide to Performance Appraisals
Living Your Dreams

Dale has also authored a variety of business programs including:

7 Steps to Becoming INVALUABLE
The Changing Face of Competition
From Specialist to Generalist: A Transition Every Business Leader MUST *Make*
Beyond Demographics: A Values-Based Approach to Marketing
Making the EXCEPTIONAL Normal

All of these programs have one thing in common. They are based on the skill of counter-intuitive thinking, a way of thinking that is contrary to what our human nature suggests. Counter-intuitive thinking allows you to see opportunities that others don't see and find solutions that are simple, inexpensive, and easy to implement.

To see how counter-intuitive thinking can be applied to everyday problems, visit Dale's Invaluable Leader Blog at www.furtwengler.com/theinvaluableleader/. If you'd like to receive email reminders for The Invaluable Leader blog, send Dale an email at dale@furtwengler.com and include the words "Invaluable Leader reminder" in the subject line.

For more information on Dale, his books, and his programs, visit
www.furtwengler.com or call him at 314-707-3771.

Look for These Best-Selling AMACOM Titles
at www.amacombooks.org

Building a Winning Sales Force by Andris A. Zoltners, Prabhakant Sinha, and Sally E. Lorimer $34.95

Delivering Knock Your Socks Off Service, 4th Edition by Performance Research Associates $18.95

Digital Engagement by Leland Harden and Bob Heyman $24.00

Get Clients Now™, 2nd Edition by C. J. Hayden $19.95

Knock Your Socks Off Prospecting by William "Skip" Miller and Ron Zemke $16.95

Questions that Sell by Paul Cherry $16.95

Red-Hot Cold Call Selling, 2nd Edition by Paul S. Goldner $17.95

The Accidental Salesperson by Chris Lytle $17.95

The Secrets of Word-of-Mouth Marketing by George Silverman $17.95

Selling to Anyone Over the Phone by Renee P. Walkup and Sandra McKee $14.95

Web Copy that Sells, 2nd Edition by Maria Veloso $21.95

Available at your local bookstore, online, or call 800-250-5308.

Savings start at 40% on bulk orders of 5 copies or more!
Save up to 55%!
Prices are subject to change.